Changing
Jersey City

A History In Photographs

Cynthia T. Harris and Leon Yost ◇◇◇◇◇ Foreword by John Gomez

Schiffer Publishing Ltd

4880 Lower Valley Road · Atglen, PA · 19310

Other Schiffer Books on Related Subjects

Jersey City: A Monumental History, 978-0-7643-2638-7, $24.95
Atlantic City, 1854-1954: An Illustrated History, 978-0-7643-3187-9, $24.99
Sea Isle City Remembered, 978-0-7643-3126-8, $19.99
Plainfield, New Jersey's History and Architecture, 978-0-7643-2915-9, $29.99

Schiffer Books are available at special discounts for bulk purchases for sales promotions or premiums. Special editions, including personalized covers, corporate imprints, and excerpts can be created in large quantities for special needs. For more information contact the publisher:

Published by Schiffer Publishing Ltd.
4880 Lower Valley Road
Atglen, PA 19310
Phone: (610) 593-1777; Fax: (610) 593-2002
E-mail: Info@schifferbooks.com

For the largest selection of fine reference books on this and related subjects, please visit our web site at: **www.schifferbooks.com**
We are always looking for people to write books on new and related subjects. If you have an idea for a book please contact us at the above address.

This book may be purchased from the publisher.
Include $5.00 for shipping.
Please try your bookstore first.
You may write for a free catalog.

In Europe, Schiffer books are distributed by
Bushwood Books
6 Marksbury Ave.
Kew Gardens
Surrey TW9 4JF England
Phone: 44 (0) 20 8392 8585; Fax: 44 (0) 20 8392 9876
E-mail: info@bushwoodbooks.co.uk
Website: www.bushwoodbooks.co.uk

Designed by RoS
Type set in Brush Script MT/Souvenir Lt BT
ISBN: 978-0-7643-3363-7

Printed in China

Dedication

To all of you who have, at one time or another, called Jersey City home and, most especially, to the students of PS # 14 and 27. You will always have a place in our hearts.

Acknowledgments

Jersey City is comprised of neighborhoods containing more than 200 citizens' associations, including block-watch groups, historic associations, park associations, church groups, and citywide coalitions. Much of this book evolved from slide talks and valuable feedback from these active groups over the last twenty years; they include: the Van Vorst Park, Harsimus Cove, and Hamilton Park Neighborhood Associations; Historic Paulus Hook Association; the Riverview Neighborhood and Sergeant Anthony Park Associations; the Communipaw Avenue Block and Madison Avenue Associations; Jersey City Women's Club and Jersey City AARP; Grace Seniors; the Village Neighborhood Association; North District Police Department; Hudson County Genealogical Society; the Jersey City Museum; the Jersey City Free Public Library and its following branches, Heights, Miller, Greenville, and Five Corners; the Jersey City Landmarks Conservancy; Hudson Artists of New Jersey; Saint Peter's Preparatory School; Danforth Avenue Neighborhood Association; Grandview Tenants; Saint Aeden's Rosary Group, Our Lady of Mount Carmel Rosary Society, and Our Lady of Fatima Society of Saint Nicholas Church.

We recognize the role of the countless collectors and dealers who, at one time or another, assisted us both in expanding our collections and finding elusive, unique images to inspire us further. We offer a special salute to Hoboken's George Kirchgessner (1919-2001).

Also essential to this book are authors and webmasters who set high standards and professional precedents. Several who are currently active include Joan Doherty Lovero, Patrick B. Shalhoub, Kenneth French, Randall Gabrielan, Charles P. Caldes, and Carmela A. Karnoutsos. Additionally we thank Peter Zirnis, who coined the term "The Architectural Landscape" for a documentary photographic exhibition in 2002; Jeff Wenger of the Jersey City Division of Planning and David Donnelly of the Mayor's Office, both of whom generously supplied up-to-date statistical information, and preservation specialist Ulana Zakalak provided crucial historical information. Photographer Alton O'Neill, also of the Mayor's Office, provided official city photographs.

We extend gratitude to Alan Delozier and Kathleen S. Dodds of Seton Hall University Archives & Special Collections Center, Mary Kinahan-Ockay of Saint Peter's College Archives and Photographic Collection, and Neal Brunson of the Afro-American Historical Society Museum. Thanks also to Claire Wilson of the Cemetery Department of the Town of Oxford, Massachusetts and Jean O'Reilly of the Oxford Historical Commission.

A special thanks to Erna MacGregor for steadfastly searching through microfilm; Ana and Reynoldo, Walgreen's digital photo specialists, for their patience and interest in assisting a neophyte; Jacqueline Wisner, for her hunting skills; and, finally, to Brittany Marie Harris and Eleen Peterson for their unflagging encouragement and support.

An especially sincere thanks goes to John Gomez, the irrepressible activist and professionally credentialed preservationist who founded the Jersey City Landmarks Conservancy and writes the "Legends and Landmarks" column for *The Jersey Journal*. Not only does John set the highest standards for preservation, but he also inspires curiosity and professionalism among his gifted students in the Jersey City Public Schools as well as the broader public through his thought-provoking walking tours sponsored by the Jersey City Landmarks Conservancy.

We thank our editors at Schiffer Publishing, Tina Skinner and Jennifer Marie Savage, for their patience with our protracted progress. They never gave up on us and for that we are grateful. Heartfelt thanks to our spouses, Erma Martin Yost and Bernard W. Harris for their patience, perseverance, and proofreading during the long writing process.

Finally, we humbly acknowledge those God-given gifts that enabled us to bring this project to fruition.

Contents

Foreword

This is the illustrated history book we have been waiting for.

Changing Jersey City: A History in Photographs, authored and imaged by Cynthia Harris and Leon Yost, takes the captioned photo and postcard genre — made widely popular in the last decade by small independent presses — to a new level. How could it not, with the indefatigable Cynthia Harris, manager of Hudson County's main historical research repository, the New Jersey Room, tapping into its voluminous archival compendiums? And what of the commanding photographic contributions of Leon Yost, also known widely throughout the city as an ardent preservationist, dedicated planning board commissioner, spirited slide-talk lecturer, and prescient proponent of the arts since the early 1970s?

All this — and the fact that both authors possess prized personal postcard collections — adds up to an accomplished document. *Changing Jersey City* is a virtual visual presentation that follows, in a panoramic arc, the palpable and the indefinable — namely, the city's built vernacular heritage and its compelling social legacy, from the formative decades of the seventeenth century up to the postmodern present. Harris and Yost divide this arc into two distinct yet linked sections. Chapters one, two, and three, researched and written by Yost, highlight Jersey City's colloquial architectural landscape, including such stately seminal icons as City Hall, the Justice William J. Brennan, Jr. Courthouse, and the former Jersey City Medical Center. Chapters four, five, and six, composed by Harris, focus on "the human face" of the municipality — the actual city street, be it cobbled or blacktopped; the century-old school house, its cavernous classrooms and stained-glass auditoriums still alight with lectures and laughter; and the eclectic assortment of people who experienced life on the stoop and never forgot it.

We are fortunate to have these two academic forces put their knowledge and passion down on paper. Though worthy of serious scholars and historians, *Changing Jersey City* is invariably aimed at the general public — an appreciative readership eager for fresh historical information, never-before-seen archival views, and superb color photography, all bountifully provided here by the authors. Undoubtedly, local educators and students will refer to it for lessons and school reports; seniors and long-time residents will ponder featured sites, both familiar and close to their hearts; newcomers will discover monuments right next door; and property owners will learn about the significance of the landmarks they've invested in.

The best history books provide intriguing facts and answers; they provoke reflections and ruminations; they send readers, in this case, out into the street, beyond the book stack and reading table, to experience the historical resource up close—and *Changing Jersey City*, the bound radiant result of a professional collaboration, triumphs in that literary duty.

John Gomez,
Columnist, *The Jersey Journal*
Founder, Jersey City Landmarks Conservancy

This is Jersey City's signature "Gold Coast" just before dawn on a cold morning in March 2007. The 781-foot-tall Goldman Sachs tower (2004), designed by Cesar Pelli, anchors the left, the Exchange Place fills the center, and the Newport mixed-use development tapers off to the right. The fifty-foot diameter Colgate Clock gently illuminates the far left on the site of the future "Veterans' Park" while Hoboken's Lackawanna RR Terminal is faintly visible on the extreme right. The Lackawanna is the last of the great railroad terminals on the lower Hudson still operating in its original function.

On May 23, 1857, *Ballou's Pictorial* published this illustration of the same busy Jersey City waterfront. Sailboats and steamboats crowd the Hudson in front of the New Jersey Railroad Terminal (later the Pennsylvania) at Exchange Place (center).
Courtesy of the Jersey City Free Public Library.

VIEW OF JERSEY CITY, N. J., FROM THE RIVER.

Chapter One:

The Changing Skyline

From the moment Henry Hudson (1570-1611) laid anchor near Communipaw Cove on September 12, 1609, and declared it "as pleasant a land as one need tread upon," Jersey City has never stopped changing. Four hundred years later, her signature skyline boasts New Jersey's tallest tower, which, at the time of this writing, is the nation's largest, certified environmentally friendly structure. It punctuates the rapidly expanding spectrum of postmodern skyscrapers that are doubly branded the "Gold Coast" and "Wall Street West." This financial powerhouse was envisioned by founding father Alexander Hamilton (1757-1804), who said, "One day a great city will rise on the west bank of the Hudson River." Although legendary Mayor Frank J. Hague — christened Francis Joseph Hague but later changed to Frank (1875-1956) — sought to entice Wall Street traders to Jersey City in the 1930s, it was not until the 1980s that they finally arrived following the adaptive renovation of the Pennsylvania Railroad's Harborside Terminal and the newly built skyscrapers, 10 Exchange Place (aka Exchange Place Center) and 101 Hudson Street.

South of the Gold Coast is Jersey City's "Emerald Coast," the crescent-shaped, 1,122-acre Liberty State Park that gently arcs around the historic Jersey Central Railroad Terminal, Ellis Island, and the internationally iconic Statue of Liberty.

To the north is Newport, the shopping mall, office center, and residential city-within-a-city envisioned by the late Sam Lefrak (1918-2003) in the 1970s and built in the 1980s.

The photographs in this chapter—some old, some new—document our waterfront's evolution from pastoral colony to industrial port to financial powerhouse.

The first Colgate Clock was installed on top of a now-demolished Colgate building in 1908. Its octagonal shape was a branding statement for Colgate's Octagon soap. At 38-feet in diameter, it was the world's largest at the time, visible from a distance of four miles. In this photograph, workmen climb the fifty-foot replacement that was installed in 1924.

This real photo postcard shows the soon-to-be-installed minute hand of the clock in a parade passing City Hall in 1908.

Built in 1891, the Pennsylvania Railroad's grand glass passenger terminal was, at the time, the largest in the world at 110 feet high, 256 feet wide, and 652 feet long. Twelve trains could enter side by side, and like a mammoth umbrella, natural light entered while rain was kept out. Rushing passengers would quickly and comfortably transfer either to the ferries, or after 1908, to the Hudson and Manhattan tubes. *(Circa 1910)*

Today, New York Waterway navigates the same waters as the Pennsylvania ferries did. The green glass-skinned, 490-foot tall office tower at 10 Exchange Place (aka Exchange Place Center) now occupies the footprint of the former Pennsylvania Terminal. Designed by Grad Associates and built from 1986 to 1989, this was the first truly Postmodern skyscraper on the Jersey City waterfront. It fittingly filled the site of the 1891 arced-glass Pennsylvania passenger terminal. That terminal, which was modeled after a pavilion in the 1889 Paris Exposition, was also designed in the newest style of architecture of its time. *(January 2004)*

Photographed on April 13, 2000, this aerial view looks westward, showing the former Colgate Palmolive industrial complex. To the far right, 90 Hudson Street is already complete, and second from right, 70 Hudson is under construction. Directly behind 90 Hudson is the last remaining Colgate building, the adaptively renovated Merrill Lynch building, on Greene Street between York and Grand streets. To the left, the Colgate clock temporarily rests where the foundation for the new Goldman Sachs tower will soon be laid. Further to the left are the Little Basin and the later Big Basin of the historic Morris Canal.

Looking northeast in February 2002, the Goldman Sachs tower begins to rise on the southern tip of Paulus Hook. To its left, the twin Liberty Towers, designed by Gruzen Samton Steinglass, are also under construction. In the left background, the cube-shaped Harborside Plaza Five, designed by Grad Associates, has just topped off.

By October 2002, Plaza Five and Liberty Towers are completed and the reflective glass curtain wall of the Goldman Sachs Tower has climbed more than halfway to the top.

< Aptly named Portside, this Mobil and Gulf petroleum tank farm covered the peninsula between the Big and Little basins of the Morris Canal. *Jersey City Planning Division photo, 1954, Courtesy of the Jersey City Free Public Library.*

> Today the same piece of land is completely transformed. Where the tanks once stood is now Liberty State Park North. The Portside residential towers occupy the far left. Liberty Towers and the Goldman Sachs tower rise in the distant center. *(October 2006)*

This elevated-perspective artist's rendering shows the soon-to-be-built Pennsylvania Terminal at Exchange Place (subsequently the name was changed to Harborside Terminal). Constructed in 1930 with a modified design, the giant complex included a cold storage and two dry storage warehouses. Immediately to their left are the twelve-train-wide passenger tracks and the Pennsylvania Railroad's headquarters building. The "Pennsy" was the largest railroad in the world and for a time had an annual budget larger than the United States federal government. *Courtesy of the Jersey City Free Public Library.*

With the Pennsy's demise in the late 1960s, their terminal lost its original function. In the 1980s, it became Jersey City's first adaptive reuse of a major industrial complex and is renamed Harborside Financial Center. Viewed from a protruding pier, right to left, Two Harborside, One Harborside, 101 Hudson Street, 10 Exchange Place, and the Goldman Sachs tower. *(May 2004.)*

This December 3, 1930 photograph shows Pennsylvania Pier F under construction. It is the left pier of the three pictured in the prior Pennsylvania Terminal rendering.

In 2002, the Hyatt Hotel replaced the then-abandoned and dilapidated pier building. In the background, from left to right, are the green glass-skinned 10 Exchange Place and Five Harborside Plaza, both designed by Grad Associates. *(January 2004)*

Looking southeast and upward from York Street, the twin green glass towers of 77 Hudson and 70 Greene (aka the Hudson Greene, designed by Cetra/Ruddy) rise gracefully into the lower waterfront skyline. Their articulated prism-like curtain walls maximize the views for their intended upscale residents. These are among the most deluxe residences ever built in Jersey City; in 2007, a pair of penthouses at 77 Hudson pre-sold for a record $6 million. *(June 2008)*

A northwesterly view from the top of 77 Hudson Street encompasses an eclectic assortment of high-rise buildings constructed over the last fifty years. The two terracotta-colored Metropolis Towers (left center) were built in the early 1960s when protruding balconies were popular. Behind them, the light colored, five-sided One Pershing Plaza, built in 1988, introduces a suburban corporate look. In the right center, the white grid-surfaced Evertrust Plaza, built in 1986 and designed by Shoji Shimutsu, displays a sophisticated minimalist sensibility. To its left, the gray and white-layered 50 Columbus, built in 2008, was designed by Thomas P. McGinty to look like a stack of floating white cubes, a Postmodern illusionist idea. *(June 2008)*

The lower tip of the downtown waterfront was the eastern terminus of the 102-mile-long Morris Canal from its opening in 1836 to 1923, when it was officially abandoned. This c. 1900 view shows a canal boat in Lock 22E. The lock is now encapsulated beneath the intersection of Washington and Dudley streets in Paulus Hook. Only ten feet wide at these narrow locks, the canal was a carefully engineered sliver of water stretching across the entire state of New Jersey and ending on the Delaware River at Phillipsburg. It mainly carried coal that was floated down the Lehigh River and Lehigh Canal from the mines of northern Pennsylvania. *Courtesy of The Morris Canal, James Lee, 1979.*

In July 1970, the World Trade Center towers were under construction and the Little Basin had evolved into the Greene Street Boat Basin, a rent-free shantytown for boaters with electricity conveniently "borrowed" from nearby utilities. *Courtesy of the Jersey City Free Public Library.*

In the 1950s, documentary photographer Dan McNulty (1907-1976) took this picture from inside the now-abandoned canal lock. By this time most of the canal was filled in, but the Little Basin remained a holding place for boats and barges. *Courtesy of the Jersey City Free Public Library.*

The low-rise downtown houses crouch below the tall office towers along the fast growing waterfront. Viewed from the top of Murdoch Hall in January 2004, the just completed new Medical Center on Grand Street is visible on the far right of this panoramic view. The old Medical Center dominated Jersey City's skyline for more than half of the twentieth century, but now its Deco-style rooftops offer the perfect vantage from which to view the new skyline that seems to merge seamlessly into lower Manhattan.

In March 1996, the Twin Towers dominated the eastern view from the Little Basin. Fresh snowfall and dry winter air created a crisp, clear vista making Manhattan seem closer than its actual 1.5-mile distance. The redbrick residential building on the left is Clermont Cove, an industrial warehouse adaptively renovated in the 1980s.

Just before dawn September 12, 2001, another clear morning reveals smoke drifting silently southward from the former Twin Towers the day after the terrorist attacks that rocked the nation. Like slow motion through a sound-damping prism, those tragic events stunned transfixed friends, neighbors, and families who knew that their lives from that moment on were forever changed.

Jersey City's upper waterfront extends northward from the Exchange Place financial district to Hoboken's southern border. Once this was the busy end-of-the-line for the Erie Railroad, but wasted and abandoned after her operations ceased in 1958, the strategically located, attractively priced land proved irresistible to Newport's redevelopers two decades later.

The Erie Railroad stockyards and passenger facilities laid claim to Jersey City's upper waterfront from 1852 to 1958. Famous for timeliness, the Hamilton Watch Company even used the Erie in its advertisements in the 1920s: boasting "a train every 100 seconds," it implied that such precision required an accurate Hamilton watch. This easterly view shows the passenger sheds and terminal at the foot of Pavonia Avenue. Their stockyards, just south of Fifth Street, were the largest east of Chicago. *Kalmbach Publishing Company, 1946.*

This April 13, 2000 aerial view shows the terminal area that has since become the Newport residential community, shopping mall, and office center. The box-like Newport Office Center One in the distance stands on the land where Erie trains pulled into the passenger terminal until 1958.

Today the foot of Pavonia Avenue, where the passenger sheds formerly stood, is Newport's Town Square Park. This January 2005 view shows the trees decorated with annual holiday lights.

The last relic of the Erie Railroad at Newport is the letter "E" formed into each of the cast-iron capitals of the PATH station's support columns. These columns were installed c. 1908 by the Hudson and Manhattan Railroad when they completed the first trans-Hudson tunnel and created this underground station to allow easy transfers from the Erie Terminal above. *(May 2002)*

PAVONIA NEWPORT

Extending southward from the Exchange Place financial district, Liberty State Park's level land was largely created by earthen fill dumped into an extensive maze of wooden cribbing sunk into the Hudson River by the Jersey Central Railroad in the late nineteenth century. This newly created land allowed the Jersey Central to create the Communipaw Yards, the largest on the Hudson with 118 miles of track. The main visual features of the Jersey Central's landscape were two round engine houses — one for passenger and one for freight engines — coal dumpers and float bridges, and the immense passenger terminal with its train-sheds, ferry-slips, and Eclectic Victorian main hall. Only the passenger terminal remains today, managed and partially restored by the State of New Jersey. The Liberty Science Center was built on the footprint of the passenger engine house and the Hudson Waterfront Walkway replaced the coal dumpers and float bridges. Jersey City's last functioning float bridge still operates several times a week in the Greenville Yards, another freight terminal some 0.5 miles south of Liberty State Park.

Off the coast in the harbor are the two other main attractions of Liberty State Park, completing the historic trilogy of the Jersey Central Terminal: Ellis Island and the Statue of Liberty. These attractions plus the busy Liberty Science Center make Liberty State Park the most visited in New Jersey by more than four million people every year.

A worldwide emblem of freedom, the iconic Statue of Liberty, under a rising full-moon and viewed from the southern Waterfront Walkway in Liberty State Park, rivals the grandest views found anywhere on the planet. *(May 2004)*

"When you're looking at the Statue of Liberty, you are looking at Jersey City," is a saying authenticated by this c. 1950 linen postcard by Alfred Mainzer. You can easily see Jersey City's smoky railroad terrain just behind the outward-gazing Miss Liberty. From Jersey City's side, you'll sometimes hear, "Her back is toward us because she trusts us!"

Nearly every type of aircraft has at sometime encircled the Statue since her official unveiling on October 28, 1886. This 1931 view shows a six-prop DO-X seaplane flying closely over the island.

A visit to Liberty Island was a rite of passage for many, as documented by photo concessionaires who merged tourists with the Statue via in-camera paste-ups that allowed sunny prints regardless of the weather or time of day. This well-dressed circa Roaring Twenties couple might well be on a honeymoon to Jersey City. French sculptor Frédéric Auguste Bartholdi (1834-1904) spent fifteen years creating the Statue, which an acquaintance said was modeled after his mother's face.

The formal structures on Ellis Island were designed to impress the sea-worn immigrants who passed through her super-sized doors. Fittingly, fireworks each Independence Day add to the impressive grandeur. The United States Supreme Court awarded eighty-nine percent of the Island to New Jersey in 1998 because the greatly enlarged land was created with New Jersey fill. The restored main building reopened in 1990 and plans are slowly underway to restore the remainder of the Island, making this a comprehensive museum of American immigration. (July 4, 2004)

My dear Bess — Don't forget to let me know when you are coming in, I am so anxious to see you, ha ha! Love, Martha

Aug 9. 1906

Hope you are well and having an enjoyable time.

Copyright 1906 by the Rotograph Co.
A 82 b. Immigrant Station, Ellis Island, N. Y. City.

Opened in 1892, the Great Hall majestically rises from the harbor where steamers dock in 1906. The arched entrances combine with upper-story windows to make them appear even larger than their actual larger-than-life dimensions. *The Rotograph Company, New York. Circa 1906.*

Natural light fills the Great Hall, or Registration Room, in this 1905 postcard view from the upper balcony. Immigrants proceed through gated corridors to checkpoints manned by uniformed officials. By 1954 when it closed, some 12 million immigrants had registered, making this the largest immigration destination in the history of the world to that time. More than 100 million Americans can trace their roots to these doors. *The Rotograph Company, New York.*

U. S. IMMIGRATION STATION, ELLIS ISLAND, NEW YORK.

RAILROAD TICKET ROOM.

Huddled masses, including many small children, timidly wait in the railroad ticket room in this 1925 hand-colored postcard. Worldly possessions are packed and bundled in boxes by their sides. *D. T. Magowan, Maplewood, New Jersey.*

Viewed from exactly the same spot ninety-nine years later, the restored Great Hall looks nearly the same, although it's missing the original divided corridors and benches. *(August 2004)*

The Jersey Central Railroad Terminal completes the historic trilogy of Liberty State Park. The terminal was constructed in three attached parts: the expansive train shed, the two-story ferry house and the three-story head house or main building. Here, the red brick head house is viewed from the harbor in dramatic morning light. Its architectural style is Eclectic Victorian, designed by Peabody & Stearns and the Jersey Central's engineers. Abandoned when the Jersey Central ceased operations in April 1967, it was restored in the 1980s and 1990s to become the last surviving major passenger terminal in Jersey City. *(May 2001)*

Preserved on film in Barbra Streisand's memorable "Funny Girl" scene in the 1960s, the train shed was the largest of its kind in the world when it opened in 1914. Designed by the Lackawanna Railroad's Chief Engineer, Lincoln Bush (1860-1940), who also designed Hoboken's Lackawanna train shed, it is 818 feet long and 370 feet wide, large enough to accommodate twenty trains side by side. At its peak, up to four hundred trains used this facility every working day. *Courtesy of the Jersey City Free Public Library.*

In this June 1963 photograph, the crowded ferry *Wilkes-Barre* arrives from Liberty Street in Manhattan, gently navigating the smooth waters into the open ferry slip. The valuable copper-clad ferry-house would soon disappear and today we are left with only the massive wooden pilings and passenger bridges.

A Jersey Central diesel rotates on the turntable of the engine house. *The Port of New York Authority, March 5, 1957.*

Like beads on many slender threads, coal cars line the tracks of the southern Communipaw freight yards. Two white plumes of smoke date this easterly view to the steam era of the early twentieth century.
Circa 1940, Fairchild Aerial Surveys.

<

This c. 1960 aerial photo looks southward toward the Jersey Central's engine-house nestled within the maze of tracks that comprise the northern Communipaw Yards. The Big Basin of the Morris Canal is on the bottom and the New Jersey Turnpike extension on the right. Today the Liberty Science Center (1993) stands on the footprint of the engine-house.
Courtesy of the Jersey City Free Public Library.

>

On a cold winter morning the Liberty Science Center rises like a multi-faceted crystal from the now forested rail yards. *(January 2001)*

Chapter Two:

The Iconic Buildings

Today some 40,000 buildings make up Jersey City, but we have singled out these few iconic examples for their storied histories and architectural significance. City Hall is the seat of government, the Hudson County Courthouse is the seat of justice, and the mammoth Jersey City Medical Center was the place where countless residents were born and cared for from the cradle to the grave.

City Hall

The cornerstone for the new City Hall at 280 Grove Street was laid at noon on May 26, 1894. Construction was completed January 1, 1896, but the official opening was not until January 18, 1897. Jersey City's official architect of the time, Lewis H. Broome (1849-1927), designed the eclectic, classically derived building with a square block-like base and middle that supported five towering copper cupolas. The opening was delayed after Broome was indicted for allowing inferior building materials. According to the *New York Times*, "He was both surprised and indignant that he should have been indicted, and says that he will be able to show what he did to protect the public interests." The cost of the building and land was $736,267. *Circa 1907, John C. Voigt, Jersey City.*

Jersey City's first City Hall stood on a now-erased street grid at the southwest corner of Newark Avenue and Coopers Alley, a block east of the present City Hall, where the Metropolis Towers stand today. It was completed in 1861 for $135,145. Prior to its construction, government business was conducted at various taverns and halls. This view of the symmetrically proportioned, classically inspired building appears to be taken near the time it opened. *Courtesy of the Jersey City Free Public Library.*

Truncated today, the aesthetically diminished City Hall survived 112 years of battles both inside and outside its doors. In the background, the blandly modern 1988 Pershing office building rises on the site of the former Grove Street ShopRite. Just beyond that, the chunky modern Grove Pointe residential building opened in 2007.

Armistice Day, November 11, 1918, marked the end of the Great War and was probably the first major international event celebrated at the new City Hall. Viewed from in front of the Majestic Theater across Grove Street, the excited crowd clamors in Hague-era exuberance. *Courtesy of the Jersey City Free Public Library.*

In a tradition that began in the nineteenth century, each New Year's Day supporters could personally meet and congratulate the Mayor without going through the usual protocols. This image, taken January 1, 1949, documents the long line of well-wishers waiting to enter City Hall. By 1949, Frank Hague was no longer Mayor, but his nephew, Frank Hague Eggers (1901-1954), held the office until his defeat by John V. Kenny (1894-1975) later the same year. The Mayor's office is in the second-story right corner. *Courtesy of the Jersey City Historical Project.*

On April 5, 1955, Mayor Bernard J. Berry (1913-1963) and Commissioner of Parks, Joshua Ringle (c. 1891-1960), "modernized" City Hall by removing the five towering copper copulas. City records were stored in these copulas, accessible only by ladder from the outside. Commissioner Ringle, a roofer, argued emphatically for the removal, convincing his fellow City Commissioners that the copulas had no functional or aesthetic value. According to *The Jersey Journal*, he said, "We'll find a storage place for the records before we knock off those ugly towers."
From the Dan McNulty Collection. Courtesy of the Jersey City Free Public Library.

This news wire photograph shows the two officials most responsible for removing City Hall's copulas. Commissioner Ringle is signing a contract; the well-dressed Mayor Berry is third from the left. For this occasion the Mayor and Commissioner are in the Council Chambers approving a contract with the Brooklyn Dodgers to play an exhibition game and seven league games in Roosevelt Stadium.
January 24, 1956, International News Photos.

These skeletal ruins remained until a wooden roof was erected over the burned section. The building stayed in this "temporary" condition until partial restoration was begun in 1995.
Courtesy of the Jersey City Free Public Library.

On September 12, 1979, while City Hall was undergoing restoration, fire erupted from paint containers, destroying the north towers and pediments along with three copper allegorical friezes. Perhaps the saddest loss that day was the stained glass skylight in the rotunda said to be from Tiffany Studios.
Courtesy of the Jersey City Free Public Library.

City staff workers carry records down the water-soaked steps after the fire. Mayor Thomas F. X. Smith (1927-1996) stands at the top of the steps on the far left.
Courtesy of the Jersey City Free Public Library.

This view of the south façade and pediment was taken on a cold winter morning soon after the 1995 restoration. The sculpted frieze by William H. Mullins (d. 1932) of Salem, Ohio is an allegory to art and industry. Today, two of the original five friezes remain. *(March 1996)*

Hudson County Courthouse

The first Hudson County courthouse was a perfectly symmetrical Greek Revival structure modeled after the temples on the ancient Acropolis. Its replacement, a much larger and grander Beaux-Arts building, was designed by the talented young Hugh Roberts (1867-1928) who sought to match or surpass the best public buildings anywhere in the United States. It, like City Hall, also caused a scandal, but this was of the opposite kind. Critics blasted Roberts in the press for creating such an extravagant building and they complained that the three million dollar cost was a senseless waste of money. Once the new Hudson County Hall of Records and Administration Building opened in 1953 (and enlarged in 1964), Roberts' building was closed and boarded up for more than a decade. Then, in imminent danger of demolition, it became the catalyst that inspired Jersey City's preservation movement. It was our symbolic "Penn Station," a comparison to Manhattan's soaring glass and granite railroad terminal (1910) that inexplicably was torn down in 1963-1964, shocking preservationists worldwide into belated action. Jersey City owes a special debt of thanks to pioneering preservationists Theodore Conrad (1910-1994), Audrey Zapp, J. Owen Grundy (1911-1985), Dr. Ethel Lawner, and others who persisted until they succeeded in saving this valuable landmark.

Built in the mid-nineteenth century, the first Hudson County Courthouse is this perfectly symmetrical Greek Revival structure modeled after the temples of ancient Athens. This small mural shows the proximity of both the first and second (1910) courthouses, which stood adjacent to each other at Newark and Baldwin avenues in Jersey City until the first was replaced by a parking lot. Painted in 1910, the mural can be seen today on the second floor of the Theodore Conrad Memorial Rotunda of the second courthouse, which was renamed the Justice William J. Brennan courthouse in 1989.

This aerial photograph, taken in April 2000, shows the Brennan Courthouse and the enlarged (1964) Hudson County Hall of Records and Administration Building side by side. The steeple of Saint Joseph's Roman Catholic Church is in the left foreground and Newark Avenue runs diagonally across the right.

The International Style Hudson County Hall of Records and Administration Building, designed by Comparetto & Kenny (1953), was built just a year after the pivotal Modernist Lever House in Manhattan (1952). The Lever House is vertical while the Hall of Records is horizontal, an intriguing early reinterpretation of a style that inspired major icons of architecture such as the United Nations building in New York and others across the world.
Linen postcard by Greenville Merchandise Company, Jersey City.

That additions are not always improvements is strikingly demonstrated by this 1964 expansion to the Hall of Records. The poorly engineered piggy-back expansion not only diminished the original interlocking architectural balance, but also created an overly dense, hard to maintain legal "warehouse." Still significant for its place in architectural history, this writer advocates removing the later addition to restore the building's 1953 early Modernist design.

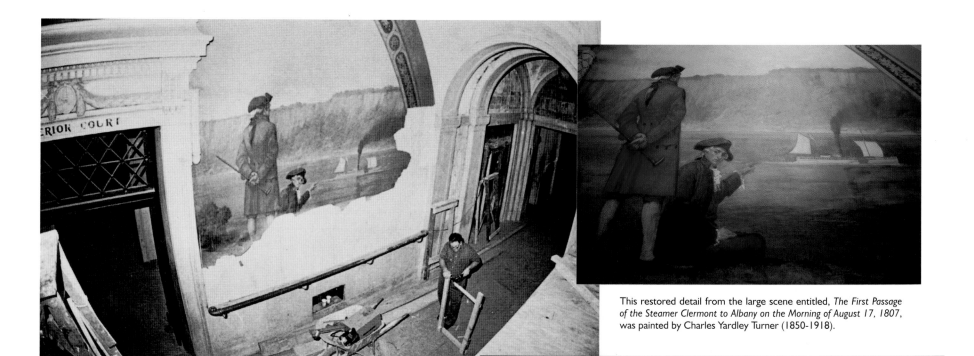

This restored detail from the large scene entitled, *The First Passage of the Steamer Clermont to Albany on the Morning of August 17, 1807*, was painted by Charles Yardley Turner (1850-1918).

Five distinguished early twentieth century American muralists and their assistants painted historical scenes on the expansive walls of the rotunda and courtrooms. During restoration, scattered fragments of the canvas-backed compositions were reapplied and the missing sections repainted. *Courtesy of the Jersey City Free Public Library.*

The twelve-segment stained glass skylight in the rotunda was severely damaged by the time restoration began in the late 1970s; it was created by F. E. Freund, who opened a stained glass studio in West Hoboken after apprenticing for Louis Comfort Tiffany (1848-1933). Adding to the insult of neglect, a shoddy roofing subcontractor threw roofing materials through it to the floor far below during restoration according to Preservationist and historian Theodore Conrad's family stories. Stained glass artist and conservationist, Charles Barone, and his team of workers completely removed and restored the damaged skylight to its perfect condition seen today. *February 1975. Courtesy of Charles Barone.*

Painstakingly polished marble finishes surround all four floors of the cavernous rotunda. *(January 2006)*

27

Jersey City Medical Center

Although the sick, injured, and inebriates were cared for in publicly managed houses from 1805 onward, it was not until 1906, under the popular young Mayor Mark M. Fagan (1869-1955), that construction of the first large public hospital began. Opened in 1909 under Fagan's successor, Mayor H. Otto Wittpenn (1871-1931), this facility anticipated what would ultimately become the nation's premier teaching hospital, a ten-building high-rise medical metropolis envisioned and completed by Fagan's political rival, Mayor Frank Hague. Hague's Jersey City Medical Center replaced Fagan's 1909 building as well as a nearly identical twin that opened c. 1919. Building the Medical Center was a logical endeavor for Hague, who from childhood constantly worried about cleanliness and cold drafts. He oversaw every detail of construction and his favorite architect, John T. Rowland, Jr. (1871-1945), designed eight of the ten buildings. Hague kept an office there and even today retired nurses tell of his midnight walks down the hospital's polished corridors, inspecting to make sure that everything was in proper order.

Built at the height of the Great Depression, in part with federal funds from Franklin D. Roosevelt's New Deal, the Medical Center became Hague's greatest bricks-and-mortar legacy. Preservationists note the irony that although Hague was no preservationist — if anything, he was anti-preservation, tearing down early Dutch houses at Bergen Square and significant structures across the city — the preservation movement and historic tax credits helped save his crowning achievement from the waiting wrecking ball.

Overbuilt from the beginning, the massive masonry city-within-a-city was expensive to operate and difficult to adapt to the twentieth century's fast changing medical technology. In recent years, only five of the buildings remained in active use for medical purposes while major buildings—the Margaret Hague Maternity Hospital, Pollak Hospital for Chest Diseases, and the East Hall nurses' residence—lay boarded and abandoned.

In 2004, an unexpected positive twist of fate forever changed the future of the Medical Center buildings. The Center became the nation's largest tax credit historical restoration project after Metrovest Equities, a real estate investment and development company, purchased the entire complex and began the adaptive renovation into modern condominium housing. The first two buildings to be renovated, the Medical Building and the Center Building (aka buildings B and C, now renamed the Capital and the Rialto), opened to their new residents in late 2007.

Hague's Democratic machine helped Franklin D. Roosevelt win the national election in 1936 and Roosevelt paid back the favor with federal funding to assist with the Medical Center's construction. Money was power, especially during the Great Depression, and — between the Medical Center, Roosevelt Stadium, and other public works projects — Hague controlled as many as 18,000 jobs, making his machine ever more invincible. In this *International News* photograph. Roosevelt ceremonially cements the cornerstone into the Medical Building at Baldwin Avenue on October 2, 1936.

You are looking at Jersey City's first large hospital building perched on the brow of Bergen Hill at Baldwin Avenue and Montgomery Street. Designed by Clinton and Russell, construction began in 1906 under Mayor Mark M. Fagan; it was completed in 1909 under Fagan's successor, H. Otto Wittpenn. This idyllic c. 1910 view looks southwest, across a small meadow, from the vicinity of Cornelison Avenue and Montgomery Street. *Courtesy of the Jersey City Free Public Library.*

This 1937 view shows Mayor Hague's much more grandiose Medical Center approaching its final form. The Medical Building (background) is topped off and the Clinic Building attached to its left is just beginning the frame up. The five-story hospital building begun by Mayor Fagan in 1909 still stands between the Medical and Surgical buildings, but a tower called the Center Building soon will replace it. Murdoch Hall and the Deco style addition to the Margaret Hague have yet to break ground. *Fairchild Aerial Surveys. Courtesy of Dennis Doran.*

<
Looking west from Bright Street, this c. 1940s linen postcard shows the freshly completed and still pristine Medical Center as Mayor Hague envisioned it. *Frank E. Cooper, New York.*

>
Photographed from an upper window of the new Medical Center on Grand Street in February 2004, this cluttered view shows a half-century of encroachment around the base of the now *old* Medical Center. The Deco brick and terra cotta skyline remains, but housing projects, the New Jersey Turnpike Extension, and poorly maintained industrial buildings fill the foreground.

Embedded in terrazzo floors, bronze medallions identify several of the main Medical Center buildings. This medallion is in the lobby of the Clinic Building on Baldwin Avenue. *(May 2004)*

<

An elevated view from May 2004 looks southeast from the roof-deck of the tall Murdoch Hall nurses' residence. Shown, left to right, are East Hall, the nurses' residence, Berthold S. Pollak Hospital for Chest Diseases, and the fabled Margaret Hague Maternity Hospital that was named by Mayor Hague as a tribute to his mother. The Margaret Hague features two cornerstones, one from each of the first and last phases of construction of the Medical Center; 1929 is on the terra cotta-roofed Neoclassical section fronting on Clifton Place and 1940 is on the Deco style twin towered section fronting on Cornelison Avenue. Christian H. Ziegler (1881-1957), a thoughtfully skilled — even poetic — architect, designed both sections. Ziegler also designed the final building in the complex, Murdoch Hall (completed in 1941), and its cornerstone is also dated 1940.

John T. Rowland, Jr. designed the other eight buildings, which have cornerstones ranging from 1929 to 1936. The 510-bed Pollak Hospital (center) is the most distinctive of the entire complex for its multi-terraced roof decks. These were created so that tuberculosis patients could receive sunshine and fresh air, the preferred treatments at the time for that dreaded respiratory-crippling disease also known as "the white plague." Hague family stories say that Pollak Hospital was the only building in the Medical Center that Mayor Hague would not enter beyond the lobby because he was afraid of contracting tuberculosis.

Audiotapes, the Jersey City Historical Project.

At dawn on May 16, 2004, dozens of ambulances, many of them borrowed from surrounding hospitals, formed a non-stop caravan, transporting some three hundred patients down the hill from the old Medical Center to their freshly finished rooms in the new Medical Center on Grand Street and Jersey Avenue. The transition was completed by 1 p.m. Operating rooms in both hospitals were active during the move to accommodate any emergencies. The background buildings, left to right, are O'Hanlon Hall (aka Jones Hall and Al Blozis Hall) doctors' residence, the Surgical Building, the Center Building, and the Medical Building. This view is south across Montgomery Street.

>

Till the end, Hague's fabled office remained on the main floor of the Center Building with the hospital using it as an administrative office. A concealed door in the wood-paneled wall behind his desk allowed the sometimes-secretive Mayor to slip out undetected by those who might be waiting. The Beacon housing development that opened to residents in late 2007 restored the paneled office, adapting it into a poker room. *(January 2004)*

Skilled at the photo-op, Hague made sure that the Medical Center would become a substantial part of his desired legacy. In this c. 1930s publicity shot, he helps Santa bring Christmas gifts to a young girl in the Children's Ward. *Davis Studios, Jersey City. Courtesy of the Jersey City Historical Project.*

31

Documentary photographer Dan McNulty took the next four images showing employees at work in the Medical Center on September 24, 1956. *Courtesy of the Jersey City Free Public Library.*

Communication was essential in a major medical institution; shown, telephone operators direct phone calls and take messages.

Large washing machines process the endless flow of laundry generated by the massive Medical Center.

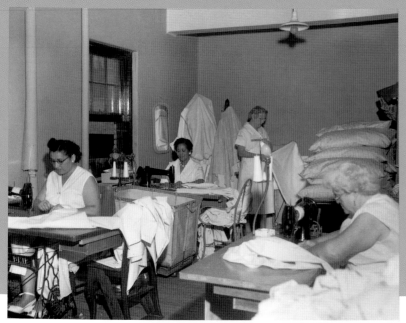

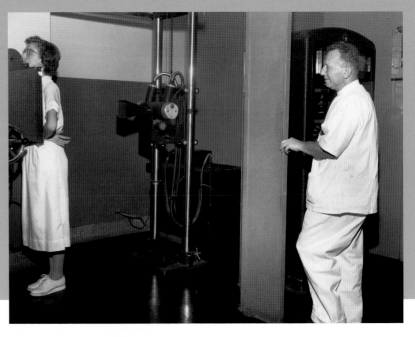

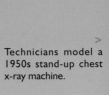

< Focused seamstresses repair clean white pillowcases using treadle-powered Singer sewing machines.

Technicians model a 1950s stand-up chest x-ray machine. >

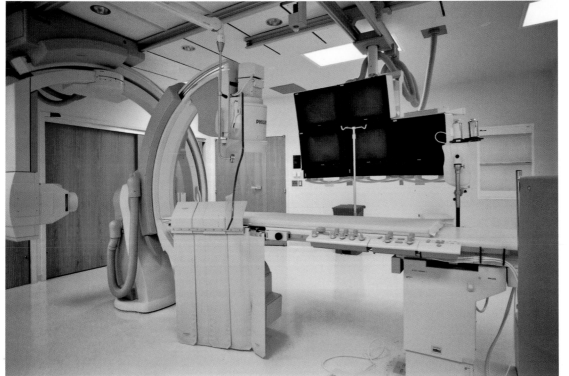

< Fifty years later, the new Medical Center boasts non-invasive surgery with real-time imaging. *(May 2004)*

> Like descending from a lighthouse tower, this long spiral staircase allowed access to the Medical Records rooms below. *(May 2004)*

> The information once contained on these shelves is now easily stored in a small computer server. *(May 2004)*

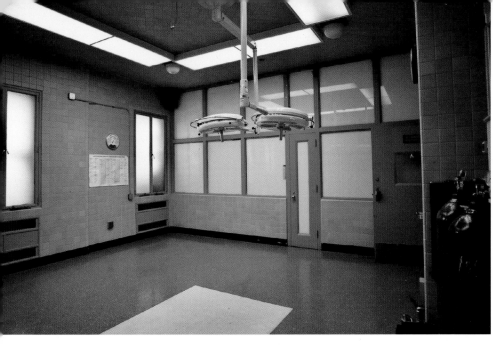

The aqua-green operating rooms were clean and operational right up until the time of the move. This large room was a teaching theater that allowed students to observe operations while seated behind the now white-painted windows on the right. *(May 2004)*

Hidden and unused for years behind tightly locked doors, the dust-covered observation gallery is a time capsule of once state-of-the-art teaching. *(May 2004)*

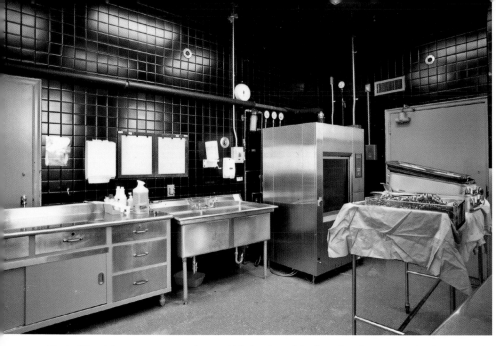

The boldly quirky aqua-green, stainless, and black colors of the Autoclave Room are strikingly modern for this 75-year-old space. *(May 2004)*

The Medical Center's morgue was in the basement of the Surgical Building. This stadium-style autopsy theater seated some fifty medical students on wooden writing chairs where they would observe instructive anatomical demonstrations. *(January 2004)*

Multiple theaters were constructed throughout the Medical Center. This Deco-trimmed example in Murdoch Hall, taken August 11, 1954, was used for lectures and nurses' entertainment. Mayor Bernard J. Berry is seated on the front row of the stage, second from right, in the inaugural ceremony for Seton Hall College of Medicine and Dentistry that would be moving into the Clinic Building in 1955. Former mayor, John V. Kenny, was in the audience.
Dan McNulty Collection. Courtesy of the Jersey City Free Public Library.

Although most of Murdoch Hall remained in good condition throughout its entire 68-year life, its ground-floor theater was closed for storage some twenty years earlier and it quickly deteriorated from roof leaks. *(October 2003)*

<

Rumors abound that hidden tunnels under the Medical Center stretch to places as distant as Dickinson High School and City Hall, allowing escape routes for those so inclined. Reality is less exciting, however, since those underground passages simply connect the various buildings carrying heat and utilities and allowing underground access by maintenance personnel. *(June 2007)*

<

An estimated 100,000 to 300,000 deliveries were performed in the Margaret Hague Maternity Hospital during its forty-eight years of operation (1931-1979). Today it is among the most deteriorated of all the major buildings. This spacious, green-tiled delivery room is typical of the hospital's debris-filled condition after fixtures and brass pipes were ripped out during the years it lay vacant to vandals. *(May 2004)*

After acquisition by Metrovest in 2004, the Jersey City Medical Center became the largest historic tax credit restoration in the United States. Shown, restoration specialists repair and re-glaze the Deco reliefs on the ceiling of the Medical Building's main floor theater. *(June 2007)*

This long east-west corridor once connected the four tall buildings known as the Clinic, the Medical Building, the Center Building, and the Surgical Building, aka buildings A, B, C, and D. With the conversion to condominiums they were renamed for famous theaters of the Art Deco era: the Mercury, Rialto, Capitol, and Orpheum. The hallway is aptly named Broadway. *(March 2008)*

Classic Deco, the bronze colored capitals and crown moldings on Broadway depict stylized ionic, acanthus, and geometric forms. Art Deco was the modern art of the Roaring Twenties, a French-inspired decorative movement that reinterpreted ancient forms into sleek machine-age designs and graphics that were quickly embraced by architecture, industry, fashion, and film. The aesthetic quickly caught on worldwide and remained popular until the 1940s. Although the movement originated in the 1920s, the Art Deco name — derived from the French *art décoratif* — was not coined until decades later in the 1960s. *(February 2008)*

Now complete, the restored theater gleams with newly polished glamour. The vintage brass fixtures were removed and restored by the world-renown Rambusch Decorating Company located just a block away on Cornelison Avenue. *(February 2008)*

Freshly restored, the capitals of the theater's square fluted Art Deco columns reinterpret ancient Greek scrolls and acanthus leaves. The colors are achieved through multiple layers of tinted glazes that create the illusion of metallic bronze and silver. *(February 2008)*

Perhaps the most significant Deco-era artwork in the Medical Center is the sculpted marble frieze inside the Baldwin Avenue entrance of the Medical Building. Some 140 feet long and five feet high, encircling the tall room just below the ceiling, the now restored frieze is entitled *From Myth to Medicine*. Under Franklin D. Roosevelt's Work Progress Administration, Allen George Newman (1875-1940) created the frieze just two years before his death. No Newman notes are known to identify the specific stories in the frieze, but he, like many artists, may have wanted the work to speak for itself. This section in the southeast corner of the room appears to depict the hand of God touching the hand of a woman. Newman, like most artists, would have studied Michelangelo's famous Sistine Chapel fresco that depicts God's hand touching Adam's, but here Newman reinterprets the scene with a personal twist, replacing Adam with a woman. *(February 2008)*

Scary mythology might describe this haunting image of *Pandora's Box*. Pandora was the Greek woman to whom Zeus gave a sealed jar for a wedding present with instructions never to open it. When curiosity eventually drove her to lift the lid, she released all the evils of the world, including disease, despair, and death. She quickly closed the lid, but only hope remained inside. *(February 2008)*

This Egyptian birth scene is on the northern wall. *(February 2008)*

The new Medical Center, at Grand Street and Jersey Avenue downtown, accepted its first patients May 16, 2004. The approximately three hundred remaining in the old multi-towered complex easily fit into this seemingly small, modern building equipped with state-of-the art imaging and non-invasive surgery, in addition to traditional technology. This image was taken from the roof of Murdoch Hall at the old Medical Center on an icy winter afternoon in January 2004. The New York Harbor in the distance is partially frozen over.

Stations of the Cross, statuary saints of healing, and candles line the rear wall of this chapel on the main floor of the Medical Building of the old Medical Center. *(February 2004)*

Reflective of today's pluralistic society, the new Medical Center's meditation chapel is a triangularly shaped, minimalist space with no overt references to any one religion. *(May 2004)*

Chapter Three:

The Architectural Landscape

Jersey City's eclectic landscape encompasses essentially five separate towns and townships that by 1873 had merged into one to make up our current municipality. At 14.9 square miles compared to Hoboken's 1.3 and Manhattan's 22, Jersey City is sufficiently large to accommodate its many "sections," all with their own individual identities. The architecture reflects this varied landscape and people. A quick walk soon reveals striking examples of the best and the worst.

Newark Avenue

Newark Avenue is the storied carriage trail that leads northwest from historic Paulus Hook, up the hill past Dickinson High School, Five-Corners, and Journal Square, through the newly invigorated Little India, and past the Marion section toward the City of Newark. Henry "Light Horse Harry" Lee (1756-1818) used part of Newark Avenue for his famous raid on the British-held fort in the swamps of Paulus Hook, the night of August 18, 1779. Newark Avenue's point of origin created a diagonal fifth corner to the intersection of Warren and Montgomery Streets. Now the first several blocks are gone — erased by the urban renewal of the early 1960s that leveled the land east of today's City Hall to make way for the high-rise Metropolis Towers (formerly the Gregory Apartments).

This c. 1910 view is looking west from Montgomery and Warren streets, toward the origin of Newark Avenue at the time. The towers of City Hall are visible in the distant left down Montgomery Street. There once was a drawbridge here that crossed a tidal creek to the swamp-surrounded sandy island of Paulus Hook. *Valentine and Sons' Publishing Company, New York.*

Today the Metropolis Towers fill the former scene, but City Hall is still visible down the widened Montgomery Street. *(January 1998)*

The intersection of Grove Street and Newark Avenue was — and continues to be — a busy one. Most of these early buildings remain, albeit missing the atmosphere of the original street lamps and giant advertising murals. A photographer with a tripod-mounted view camera is at work in the middle of the intersection while a young lady poses next to a utility pole on the far sidewalk in this pre-1908 view. *American News Company, New York.*

The modes of transportation and street lights are dramatically different, but the old cobblestones are still buried under the now asphalted Newark Avenue in this July 2006 view looking northwest.

At the triangular intersection of Bay Street, Erie Street, and Newark Avenue c. 1900, posters advertise "My Tom Boy Girl" playing at the nearby Bijou Theater. *From the Edge collection.*

Today the Morlees building (c. 1910) cuts a dramatic slice into the same easterly vista. The Beaux-Arts style New York and New Jersey Telephone Company building (now the Jersey City Police Headquarters) at Bay and Erie streets is on the left and the since restored Rocket building is on the right. *(September 1999)*

The Junction and Bergen Hill

The "Junction," located on the eastern edge of Bergen Hill next to the flat lowland neighborhood of Lafayette, may be the most complicated assemblage of intersections in all of Jersey City. Four major and five minor streets and avenues intersect here creating multiple triangular islands of land and complicated odd-shaped blocks. On the north-south axis, Summit Avenue becomes Garfield Avenue (formerly Bergen Point Plank Road), which continues south to the former Bergen Point Ferry Terminal at the tip of Bayonne. In the other direction, Summit Avenue extends northward through the Heights, ending at Paterson Plank Road on the border of Union City. The east-west axis of the Junction is Communipaw Avenue, New Jersey's oldest road and a former Lenni Lenape Indian trail. This was the short route from the clam-laden Hudson harbor across the eastward sloping maize fields to the Hackensack River. The major Grand Street thoroughfare also intersects the Junction on a northeast-southwest axis, with its name changing to Ocean Avenue at Bramhall Avenue just beyond. Prescott Street, Ivy Place, Randolph Avenue, Harrison Avenue, and Cornelison Avenue all also converge here, making the Junction the hub of a lopsided many-spoke wheel.

From c. 1865 to the early twentieth century, chemist and eccentric entrepreneur, Ephraim S. Wells (1841-1914), operated a drug manufacturing facility on the small now-vacant triangle next to the Library-Bergen Hall. Pictured are his employees lining up for a group photograph behind a horse-drawn delivery wagon. *McLean, 1895. Courtesy of the Jersey City Free Public Library.*

The five-sided former Library-Bergen Hall is the dominant structure of the Junction. It opened in the late 1860s and served as City Hall for Bergen City for less than a decade because in 1870 Bergen City merged into Jersey City. In this August 2005 northeasterly view from Summit and Communipaw avenues, National Rug and Carpet's bold white and red color scheme can be seen.

In 2007-2008, the Library-Bergen Hall was redesigned and renovated into loft-style condominiums by Minervini Vandermark Architecture. Although the decision to remove the mansard roof and add the penthouse is debatable from a pure preservation perspective, the original footprint and walls remain, effectively tying the nineteenth to the twenty-first centuries on this significant corner. (June 2008)

Victorian trade cards were popular in the 1880s and 1890s, but Wells developed his own designs and wrote his own humor. Today's paper collectors still compete for his best creations.

OUR OCCUPATION GONE "ROUGH ON RATS DID IT

A self-made businessman, E. S. Wells developed all of his own formulas — more than one hundred — and wrote all of his own advertising. In twelve years, he sold more than $2 million worth of preparations, mostly at 10-25¢.
McLean, 1895. Courtesy of the Jersey City Free Public Library.

A large lithograph, 14x21, in seven colors, of the above Rough on Rats illustration (Household Troubles), which has convulsed the world with laughter, with comic descriptive verses, mailed free.

Unbeatable Rat Exterminator
Equally Effective against Mice, Roaches, Ants and Bed Bugs

RATS and MICE instinctively avoid the familiar forms of ready prepared for use doses; Rough on Rats, the original and old reliable, being unmixed and all poison, can be disguised in many ways, thus completely outwitting them. Though a poison and originally designed for Rats and Mice, experience has demonstrated it the most effective of all exterminators of Roaches, Ants and Bed Bugs. The only thing at all effective against the large Black Cockroach or Beetle. Fools the Rats, Mice and Bugs, but never disappoints or fools the buyer. Safely used 30 years. We also make Rough on Fleas (powder), for dogs, etc., 25c.

Rough on Roaches (non-poisonous), 15c., 25c. Rough on Bed Bugs (liquid), nozzle cans, 15c., 25c.
Rough on Corns (liquid) 25c.; (salve) 15c. Rough on Corns (plasters) 8 for 10c.
Rough on Bunions remedy 35c. Rough on Bunion plasters 3 for 10c.

E. S. WELLS, Chemist   ALL SOLD BY DRUGGISTS   **JERSEY CITY, N. J., U. S. A.**

Wells soon became known worldwide for his catchy "Rough-on" advertisements, including his original Rough on Rats and subsequent Rough on Fleas, Rough on Roaches, Rough on Bed Bugs, Rough on Corns, Rough on Bunions, and Rough on Toothache. He even boasted that his products were "rough on undertakers," diminishing their livelihood by making people healthier! He spent several sleepless nights trying to name his new rat poison, but nothing he could think of sounded right. Finally, he woke up one morning saying, "Well, even if I can't think of a name for it, it certainly is rough on rats," and that's the name that stuck.

Several blocks west of the Junction, on the corner of Communipaw and Monticello avenues, the now neglected Monticello Theater tenuously survives, albeit without its original burlesque and silent film era glamour. *Circa 1914, Brooklyn Postcard Company, New York.*

E. S. Wells lived in this c. 1880 Queen Anne style Victorian mansion just up the hill from the Junction at 111 Summit Avenue. *McLean, 1895. Courtesy of the Jersey City Free Public Library.*

Times have greatly changed and now two "cookie-cutter" box houses occupy the property. Speculating developers build such houses in any available space, especially where a large house can be torn down and replaced by two. Under the rationale that "cheap sells," speculators are often proven correct by the absent aesthetic standards of many buyers. *(January 2006)*

Today a church meets upstairs while the main floor remains vacant and gated. Monticello Avenue is beginning a slow but steady rebirth with façade improvements managed by the Jersey City Economic Development Corporation with Urban Enterprise Zone funding. Potentially the theater could become the anchor for the restored commercial district much as the Hudson and Manhattan Powerhouse is the symbol of the Powerhouse Arts District. *(June 2001)*

Greenville

Easily Jersey City's largest section, Greenville is an unwieldy tract of land extending south from Myrtle Avenue to the Bayonne border. More than two miles wide, it stretches from the New York Harbor to Newark Bay, greatly enlarged by railroad fill on the east and Holland Tunnel fill on the west. In just over a century, parts of Greenville evolved from pastoral farmland to spaciously grand estates to tightly packed rowhouses to large apartment dwellings. Scattered vestiges of Greenville's earlier grandeur still survive among well-intentioned urban renewal projects and the recent clutter of "cookie-cutter" infill. Spaciously laid out, Greenville has far more avenues than streets and its greatest asset may be its potential for future "green" urban planning.

Looking northwest, this aerial view shows Greenville's southern and western boundaries. The last remaining Curries Woods high-rise is in the lower left, Country Village is in the center far left, and Society Hill, in the distant left. The curving course of the former Morris Canal cuts diagonally across the left center, traced by Route 440 and the eastern edge of Country Village. When Jersey City's eight-mile extension of the canal opened in 1836, it followed the bank of the Hackensack River separated only by a narrow dyke of land. Subsequently considerable flat land was added to its west with fill from the Holland Tunnel. The canal continued eastward, forming the border with Bayonne, then curved northward toward Lafayette, and on to its eastern terminus at Paulus Hook. *(April 13, 2000)*

Rotating the view toward the northeast, Ocean Avenue points north from the center and Garfield points northeast from the lower right. These two avenues will converge with Old Bergen Road (visible in the lower left corner) at the Bayonne border. The Ezra L. Nolan Middle School (School 40) makes up the trio of large buildings in the lower right between Ocean, Garfield, Seaview, and Gates avenues. *(April 13, 2000)*

Back of the Hill, Jersey City, N. J.

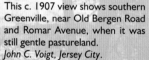

This c. 1907 view shows southern Greenville, near Old Bergen Road and Romar Avenue, when it was still gentle pastureland. *John C. Voigt, Jersey City.*

Garfield Ave., Greenville, Jersey City, N. J.

Another John C. Voigt postcard, from 1908, shows impressive Italianate and Second Empire style mansions surrounded by large lawns off Garfield Avenue. Wealthy New Yorkers built such homes in this idyllic country setting.

Raymund Roth Pioneer Home. Greenville, Jersey City, N. J.

This 1908 postcard features what is perhaps the most extravagant of all the grand houses on Garfield Avenue: the Eclectic Victorian/Shingle style Raymund Roth Pioneer Home that stood at 574 Garfield Avenue from 1887 to c. 1960. John C. Voigt took these views — many of them the best there are — during this lost era of Greenville's heyday.

Today a row of small c. 1960s homes occupy the same site, which now is named Freedom Place. *(August 2008)*

Located on the lower Hudson County Boulevard (now Kennedy Boulevard) between Gates and Seaview avenues, Armbruster's Schuetzen Park was a German restaurant, tavern, social center, and meeting place for the Greenville Camera Club, of which William Armbruster (1865-1955) was a member.
John C. Voigt, Jersey City, 1908.

Fifteen members of the Greenville Camera Club pose for this group photograph outside Schuetzen Park c. 1900. Several of them are displaying early Kodak folding cameras while one member leans on a *very* large format view camera.
Courtesy of the Jersey City Free Public Library.

This c. 1911, Fred Thoele view advertises August Lentz's horseshoe shop at 138 Ocean Avenue.

The same lower Ocean Avenue building now houses Master Kedar's Martial Arts Center while its neighbor to the right was replaced with a modern infill residence in 2007.

Kirchner's Café at 290 Jackson Avenue typifies the busy Main Street commercial character of that area c. 1908. This was the headquarters of the Jackson Avenue Social Club. *A Fred Thoele Picture.*

Following serious decline in the decades from the 1960s through the 1990s, the Jersey City Economic Development Corporation recently began façade renovations on this depressed stretch of the formerly vibrant Jackson Avenue, now renamed Martin Luther King Drive. Kim's Beauty Supply lacks the ornate leaded-glass bay windows of the former Kirchner's Café, but the building is much improved from its intervening run-down condition. *(March 2008)*

Church of the Reedeemer (Eng. Evang. Luthern) and Parsonage, Greenville. Jersey City.

The short cross-town Warner Avenue was a peaceful setting for this modestly elegant English Evangelical Lutheran Church of the Redeemer and parsonage. The shingled wood-frame structures, designed by Jersey City architects Dodge and Morrison, reflect a restrained interpretation of late nineteenth century Victorian aesthetic. *Circa 1907, F. Mansfield.*

By March 2003, the small church is enlarged, but the well-maintained parsonage is hardly changed.

This c. 1940s aerial view shows Jersey City's Roosevelt Stadium. Conceived by Mayor Hague, the stadium was a destination for sports fans from 1937 to 1978. The majestic Art Deco style arena was constructed during the Great Depression on newly-created land excavated from the Holland Tunnel (1927) and dumped into the Hackensack River on the west side of Greenville. Jackie Robinson (1919-1972) broke organized baseball's "color barrier" here on April 18, 1946, playing second base for the Montreal Royals. The stadium was demolished in 1985.
Courtesy of the Jersey City Free Public Library.

Today phase one of the Society Hill housing development occupies the Roosevelt Stadium site. This aerial view looks west from Danforth Avenue and Route 440. *(April 13, 2000)*

This western main entrance faces the Hackensack River, as photographed on the warm humid afternoon of August 16, 1957.
Dan McNulty Collection. Courtesy of the Jersey City Free Public Library.

The stadium brought Jersey City national recognition when the Brooklyn Dodgers played an exhibition and seven official league games here in 1956. The camera-loving Mayor Bernard J. Berry exploited the achievement by riding in a specially constructed parade-train to welcome the team. Seen here on Grove Street in front of City Hall, Berry waves from the engine's window.
Dan McNulty Collection. Courtesy of the Jersey City Free Public Library.

Journal Square

On the bend in the Boulevard, at the northern end of historic Bergen Avenue and above the PATH tubes to Manhattan, Journal Square is the throbbing heart of an intricate bus, taxi, and rail network. Commuters quickly pass through while nearby historic streets and avenues like Van Reypen, Academy, Tuers, and Vroom house long-time residents in rows of tidy early twentieth century houses and Roaring Twenties Deco and Tudor styled apartments. Once an entertainment center as well, the "Square" was home to Jersey City's three best-known theaters: the Loew's, the State, and the Stanley. Like New York City's Times Square, Journal Square is named for its major daily newspaper, *The Jersey Journal*, which relocated there in 1925 and still operates out of its 30 Journal Square headquarters. Despite Mayor Frank Hague's 1928 ordinance officially changing the name to "Veteran's Square" because the Journal endorsed another candidate, the original name persists, a tribute to citizens who refused to comply with a politician's self-serving agenda.

One of the New York area's five wonder theaters built specifically for "talkies," the 3,000-seat Italian Baroque Loew's Jersey came to symbolize the opulence that was Journal Square when it opened in 1929. In this Cold War era view, the United States Air Force uses the opening of "Command Decision" as a recruitment backdrop. The truck carries a World War II German V-1 Flying Bomb.
Dan McNulty, 1949. Courtesy of the Jersey City Free Public Library.

Journal Square, showing Elks Club, Universal Bldg.

and Loew's Jersey Theatre, Jersey City, N. J.

Miniature Golf on the Boulevard in Journal Square looks oddly out of place in this c. 1929 view.
Manhattan Card Publishing Company.

The large lighted Loew's Jersey sign is gone and the painted murals are faded, but the major buildings remain on this dangerously busy corner. The Loew's closed in 1986 and was slated to become a multi-story parking garage until the Friends of the Loew's convinced the city government to buy it. The Friends have since restored Loew's and it now shows vintage movies. *(July 2008)*

"The Third Man," starring Joseph Cotton (1905-1994) and Orson Welles (1915-1985), on the Loew's marquee dates this later photograph of the same corner to 1949. Now the two-story building with the famous China Clipper restaurant gently rounds the corner.
Dan McNulty Collection. Courtesy of the Jersey City Free Public Library.

In the 1930s through the 1960s, actors advertised their new releases in Journal Square's theaters. Here six mounted horsemen line up on Kennedy Boulevard for the opening of "Stagecoach" at the Fox State Theater in 1966. The State opened in 1922, making it the oldest as well as the first to be demolished of Journal Square's three great theaters.
Courtesy of the Jersey City Free Public Library.

Vacant for some two decades, Fox State Theater was demolished in 1998 and, in 2005, replaced with the twelve-story stripe-surfaced State Square apartment building designed by Peter Dewitt, AIA. *(July 2008)*

Although the exterior splendor is somewhat diminished by the loss of the large lighted rooftop billboard and the modern addition on the left, the theater was saved from an inevitable demise when Jehovah's Witness purchased and rehabilitated it after it closed to movies in 1978. It reopened as an Assembly Hall in 1985. Today free, guided tours are offered hourly through the amazingly opulent interior with its thirteen-foot tall, 45,000-piece crystal chandelier and its night-sky planetarium projected over its massive auditorium. *(March 2000)*

With a massive 4,300-seat capacity, the Stanley was not only the largest of Journal Square's theaters, but the second largest in the east after Radio City Music Hall. Designed by Fred Wesley Wentworth (1864-1943), Mayor Hague attended its gala opening in 1928. A warship with actual sailors deck-out the copper marquee for "Here Comes the Navy," starring James Cagney and Pat O'Brien, in 1934.

53

The Trust Co. of New Jersey, Jersey City, N. J.

This 1920s Fred Post postcard features the corporate headquarters for the Trust Company of New Jersey without the "Trust Company Bank" sign with its trademark two red hearts, as it had not yet been installed. Clinton and Russell designed the eleven-story Italian Renaissance style office tower that opened in January 1922 and from that day forward defined Journal Square's skyline.

Northfork Bank acquired the Trust Company's seventy-five branches in 2004 and Capital One acquired them from Northfork in 2008, subsequently updating the soaring signs on the Journal Square building. In the late 1920s, the trapezoid-shaped structure was greatly enlarged at its southern end as evidenced in this 2008 photo.

> This c. 1920s view up the Boulevard from Sip Avenue shows the attractive Seville apartment building (2801 Kennedy Boulevard), decorated with coats of arms and a gothic griffin gargoyle. The entrance is designed like a medieval walled city gate flanked by a pair of tall guard towers.

> Designed by Jersey City architect Hugh Kelly (1888-1966), the Seville is largely unchanged, but the large building at the distant corner of Tonnelle Avenue is replaced by a c. 1960s unembellished commercial structure. (October 2006)

Hudson Boulevard, Jersey City, N. J.

Mounted on top of a corner wall, this mythological flying lion — called a griffin — lends an air of protection and gothic gravitas to this extraordinary apartment building. *(June 2002)*

These are Brunswick Laundry employees — all male and probably management — circa 1920s.
PAAP Studio, Hoboken, New Jersey.

Diagonally northwest of the Square c. 1920s, Brunswick Laundry's decorated smokestack accentuated Jersey City's western skyline alongside the Pulaski Skyway for most of the twentieth century.

Sporting wide, white sidewall tires, a Brunswick Laundry delivery truck advertises diaper service in this c. 1950s image.

Today the smokestack and the lighted, three-sided billboard are both gone, leaving only the truncated base and middle. The building's sides were recently expanded to accommodate conversion to residential dwellings. *(January 2008)*

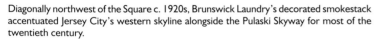

Bergen Square, Jersey City, N. J.

Bergen Square, a short walk south of Journal Square, on Bergen Avenue at Academy Street is the original village square of the first permanent settlement in New Jersey in 1660. The four-block 800 x 800-foot walled settlement was named Bergen after a small town in Holland. The 160 x 220-foot public square once contained both the village well and New Jersey's first school. This c. 1908, John Voigt view looks north across Bergen Square from Academy Street.

School 11 burned and was replaced in 1968 with a Modernist-style structure. Subsequently, its name was changed to the Martin Luther King School. The elevated gabled house still survives on the northeast corner of the square. (May 2007)

21

Scene from Bergen Square, showing Peter Stuyvesant Statue, Jersey City, N. J.

Increased density was thought to be a good thing in the early twentieth century when Jersey City was rapidly growing. In this c. 1950 view, towers make Journal Square easily visible in the distance and Deco style storefronts line the eastern side of Bergen Avenue. School 11 on the far right and the 3.5-story redbrick gabled house on the far end of the square are the lone survivors from the previous view. Close examination reveals that the gabled house was lifted from its foundation and a new first floor added underneath sometime after 1908. The Peter Stuyvesant (c. 1612-1672), aka "Peg-leg-Pete," monument, created by famed sculptor J. Massey Rhind (1860-1936), was unveiled in 1910 and is prominently featured in the lower right in front of School 11. *Greenville Merchandise Company, Jersey City.*

Established in 1868, this circa 1900 view shows workers from John M. Hughes' Sons House Raising and Moving located at Montgomery and Colgate streets (where Ferris High School stands today). That company might possibly be the one that raised the Bergen Square house, a hefty undertaking for such an unwieldy masonry structure.

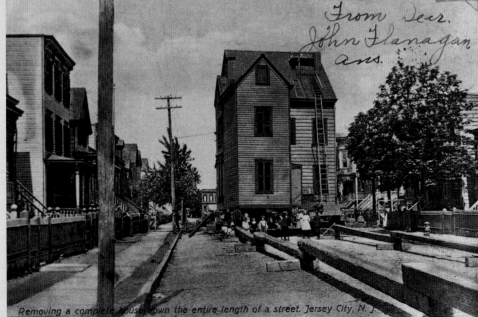

Removing a complete house down the entire length of a street. Jersey City, N. J.

In 1903, when West Side Park (now Lincoln Park) was being created, a number of homes on lower Belmont Avenue stood in the way of the 200-foot-wide approach from the Boulevard to the park. Most were demolished, but four were saved and moved to the northeast corner of Communipaw Avenue and Hudson Boulevard. Recounting her memories as an eight-year-old child, Florence Pond Graham says, "The project was breathtaking…[the houses] were put on skids and were drawn down the Boulevard by a team of mules walking in circles. We sat on the porch with our eyes popping, waiting for the flats to topple over." The houses successfully made it to their new location and stood for another half-century before finally being demolished. The wood-frame house pictured here was transported down an unknown street in Jersey City.
1907, John C. Voigt, Jersey City.

The Heights

On top of a nearly mile-wide, one hundred-foot high slab of ancient basalt formed some 190 million years ago, the Heights stretches from State Highway 139 on the south to Union City and North Bergen on the north. Geologically isolated by the Palisades cliffs on the east and the western slope on the west, the high island town was difficult to access with nineteenth century's horse-drawn carriages, wagons, and trolleys. In 1874, the *Illustrated Christian Weekly* railed that commuters from Manhattan could travel through the Erie Railroad's (1861) tunnel and ten miles into the hinterlands before Heights residents were able to make it up the cliff-clinging roads to their high homes only a short mile from the Hoboken ferries. The *Weekly* went on to point out that by the time the horses had struggled up Paterson Plank Road, they were exhausted and barely able to continue on to their nearby destinations. This would abruptly change when a two-car, steam-powered inclined elevator—480 feet long and 102 feet high—was built straight up the cliffs from Hoboken to Ogden Avenue. Designed to carry an entire team of four horses still hitched to their wagons or trolleys, this was the first elevator of its kind in the world. Not only did it make the trip faster — a remarkable one minute — but, once they reached the top, the horses were rested and ready to continue. Eventually electric trolleys and gas-powered cars and buses made the Heights more accessible, but even today this high land still has the feeling of separation from its surrounding low-lying towns and cities.

View of the Heights, Jersey City, N. J.
(Hand Painted.)

Looking northwest from southern Hoboken, this view shows the Palisades east of Ogden Avenue near Franklin Street. The switchbacks of Mountain Road go up the cliffs on the left and Paterson Plank Road heads diagonally right and upward from the lower center. The two large central buildings at the bottom of the cliffs are Sheet Iron and Plate Steel Works of L. O. Koven & Brother (aka Koven Stove Works). The Franklin Street steps (aka the "100 steps") are faintly visible on their left. On top of the cliffs, to the left, is the Jersey City Garden, a social and banquet facility with the largest ballroom in New Jersey. It advertised "home of all big dances" and "boxing every Tuesday night." *John C. Voigt, Jersey City, circa 1908.*

Three floors were added to the three Koven buildings along Paterson Plank Road in 2005-2008 when they were converted into "The Cliffs" luxury lofts. *(June 2008)*

This wider aerial view from a similar angle was taken April 13, 2000. The Koven buildings were vacated by this time, but the establishment had grown to include four redbrick buildings in the center left. The Mountain Road switchbacks are still visible on the far left and the Jersey City Garden is replaced by Harbor View Health Care Center at 178 Ogden Avenue. On top of the cliffs, to the far right, Fisk-Riverview Park is the tiny emerald oval with its gazebo a bright red dot in the center. Saint Anne's Roman Catholic Church, on the Boulevard at Congress Street, is in the far distant center.

Observer Highway in Hoboken becomes Paterson Plank Road, which climbs the cliffs, crosses the Heights, and then continues down the western slope past Secaucus on its long way to Paterson, New Jersey. In this c. 1908 view, far fewer horse-drawn carriages and wagons are climbing than are descending the long inclined road. Presumably, much of the up-going traffic has opted to ride the wagon elevator several blocks to the south. *John C. Voigt, Jersey City.*

Section of Paterson Plankroad along the Heights. Jersey City, N. J.
(Hand Painted.)

Franklin Street Steps, Jersey City down to Hoboken

The Franklin Street steps were the shortest walking route from lower Paterson Plank Road to Ogden Avenue in the Heights. This 1906 view shows the Koven Stove Works on the right and the Jersey City Garden at the upper left. *Voigt and Staeb, Jersey City.*

In this March 2001 view, the steps are gone, the Koven windows are cemented shut, and the cobblestones of Mountain Road are removed. Harbor View Health Care Center, where the Riverview Neighborhood Association holds its monthly meetings, is in the upper left.

Climbing the cliffs with a team of four horses pulling a heavy wagon was no easy task before November 21, 1874. That is the day the counterbalanced cable-pulled wagon elevator carried its first load loudly — but smoothly — up the cliffs in only a minute! This surprisingly simple design used wedge-shaped carriages on standard railroad tracks and wheels powered by steam. It was the most practical of several proposals, and amazingly, it was built in less than five months for only $80,000. On the right side of this photograph is the larger trolley trestle, built in 1886, connecting the Hoboken Terminal directly to the Heights.
Public Service Railway, January 11, 1915, North Jersey Electric Railway Historical Society, Deutsch Collection.

Viewed from the opposite direction, the 1886 trolley trestle is on the left, the 1874 wagon elevator in the center, and Pohlmann's Hall, a German social center, on the right.
Circa 1908, F. G. Temme Company, Orange, New Jersey.

Looking west from Observer Highway in Hoboken, the tree-filled space to the left of Pohlmann's Hall (upper right) is where the elevator and trestle once operated. The hefty brick and bluestone footings of the trolley trestle are still imbedded into this densely overgrown portion of the cliffs, but the only evidence of the "low tech" elevator is a graded rocky track bed. *(August 2008)*

Palisade Ave., showing Trolley Station and Public Service Building. Jersey City, N. J.

218413

This 1915 view, published by the Brooklyn Postcard Company, shows an electrified trolley entering the elevated station at Palisade Avenue and Ferry Street. When the tall trestle carried its first cars up the cliffs in 1886, it was steam driven and cable drawn. Two and a half miles of woven steel cable pulled ten cars back and forth from the Hoboken Terminal to the Heights. It's said that New Yorkers would cross the Hudson just for the ride and the unsurpassed view. Public Service Railway electrified the system a decade later, paving the way for a comprehensive trolley network that crisscrossed Jersey City's streets and those of neighboring towns. You could ride all the way to Paterson for only a nickel!

This direct photograph of the station — looking west from Palisade Avenue and Ferry Street — was taken from the catwalk between the elevated tracks. *Albert L. Creamer, July 15, 1935.*

The trolley station is replaced by a supermarket in this January 1998 photograph, but the Public Service headquarters at 325 Palisade Avenue is still the most substantial building in the neighborhood. Used for Jersey City government offices for years, the c. 1910 building was recently approved for residential conversion.

The "L" continued west to Central Avenue, where it turned south toward the Hudson County Courthouse. It's shown rounding the curve at Ferry Street and Central Avenue on the last day of operations, August 7, 1949. Looking north up Central Avenue, this view shows Saint Nicholas Roman Catholic Church in the upper right and Pershing Field on the left.

Today, that somewhat dilapidated corner has lost its central focus, which was the trolley station. The Modernist Hudson County Administration Building on the right was built in 1953 and enlarged in 1964. (February 2004)

The Central Avenue "L" descended to grade at the Court House Station at Central and Pavonia avenues. Central Avenue ends here and Summit Avenue intersects, making this a five-point intersection. Looking north from Pavonia Avenue, the distant rowhouses front on Newark Avenue. Circa 1908, Bellows & Zoaller, Jersey City.

A last physical vestige of the Central Avenue "L" is this pair of steel trestle supports located in a parking lot at Central Avenue on the north side of Newark Avenue, west of the Hudson County Administration Building. (November 2003)

THE CAR AND PASSENGER ELEVATOR, IN JERSEY CITY.

A year before the actual inclined wagon elevator was built up the Palisades, this far more expensive and difficult to build concept was published in the June 21, 1873 edition of *Scientific American*. A pair of vertical shafts would have carried counterbalanced cars sufficiently large to lift a fully loaded horse-drawn trolley or one hundred standing passengers.

One hundred and thirty years later, the present met the past when NJ Transit built this two-car passenger elevator at Hoboken's Ninth Street light rail station, connecting it to Congress Street and Paterson Plank Road in the Heights.

PATHE FRERES STUDIO, SHOWING OGDEN AVENUE, JERSEY CITY, N. J.

Although Fort Lee is the forerunner of Hollywood in early twentieth century silent films, the large French Pathé Frères Company built this studio at Ogden Avenue and Congress Street in the Jersey City's Heights. The Palisades were the "west" from the perspective of Manhattan, and westerns were filmed up and down those steep cliffs from the area around the George Washington Bridge to as far south as the low rocky terrain of Curries Woods on the Bayonne-Jersey City border.
Art Post Card & Novelty Company, Hoboken, New Jersey, 1920.

PEARL WHITE

Looking southeast from the corner of Congress Street and Ogden Avenue today, this multi-family apartment building occupies the Pathé Frères site. *(April 2006)*

Pathé Frères' star Pearl White (1889-1938) was attractive and athletic, doing her own stunts in the silent serial "The Perils of Pauline," which was filmed in and around the Palisades in 1914. In sequential episodes, Pauline would find intriguingly new ways to escape from a man who always seemed to be following her. Once she even escaped down the Palisades riding in a hot air balloon! According to the *Encyclopedia of New Jersey*, the term "cliffhanger" originated from these cliff-climbing adventures. *Circa 1910, Pathé Frères Cinema Limited, UK.*

Early postcards glamorized the Palisades as does this 1910 view of Obelisk Rock in Weehawken (with an unnamed man posing).
The Temme Company, Orange, New Jersey.

A shocking surprise, after a century of erratic encroachment, the precariously balanced Obelisk Rock is still upright, just off of Boulevard East at 51st Street on the Weehawken/West New York border. This time the man posing is Jersey City native, preservationist, and *The Jersey Journal's* "Legends and Landmarks" columnist John Gomez. *(November 2003)*

Chapter Four:

The Human Face of Jersey City

What makes a community? A city? Jersey City? Not just the bricks and mortar, nor the monuments or structures. Not just the institutions, or even the culture. In one word, it's "people." First visited by Henry Hudson in 1609 and initially settled by the Dutch shortly thereafter, Jersey City has been a mosaic of different ethnic backgrounds—the classic melting pot—as waves of immigrants from a wide array of countries from all six continents have called it home. A mere half-mile from Ellis Island meant that countless newcomers spent perhaps a year—or a generation or two—here in Jersey City before fanning out across the United States. This blending of cultures, races, and ethnicities has enriched its everyday life and contributed to making Jersey City what it is today.

These last three chapters will look at how people live, what they value, and how they established the footprints of the city. What gives them pride? And, how do they commemorate, honor, and remember the who and what that weaved together to create the culture and life that is Jersey City? While photos, maps, and written histories are the basis of preserving the past, they do not tell us much about the actual day-to-day realities of life in Jersey City. There have been occasional articles in many different publications, but two of the largest memoirs are books. Florence Pond Graham, in *Jersey City: As I Remember It,* gives us a feminine view from an affluent family living in the Bergen section. Art Wilson's book, *No Experience Required: Bumbling through Boyhood,* is from the masculine perspective of a down-to-earth middle-class family in Greenville. Their memories will sometimes be alluded to in these last chapters; after all, who better than those who lived it to describe the little day-to-day events as they really happened.

This "Greetings from Jersey City" postcard, mailed in 1908, features lovely young ladies and adorable children making up Jersey City, both literally and figuratively.

These gentlemen represent the first twenty-four mayors of Jersey City. All but the two in the center bottom row — Mark Fagan (1869-1955) and H. Otto Wittpenn (1871-1931) — were elected in the nineteenth century. *Courtesy of the Jersey City Free Public Library.*

Street Life

Everyone has to step out of his or her private domain into the world that is Jersey City. And that first step takes them into the streets. Streets, by their very nature, define the public realm of a community. The citizens are free to gather, interact with one another, and get from point A to point B within the city. Streets mark the spot — without them we would be hard-pressed to find businesses, schools, homes. Having lived on Jersey City's John F. Kennedy Boulevard, the vitality of the city can be viewed simply by peering out a window — day or night, 24/7/365.

One hundred years ago the streets were paved primarily of cobblestone with others being of granite, Belgian block, asphalt, macadam, brick, dirt, and even wooden blocks. This c. 1913 view of New York Avenue, looking north from Congress Street, shows a work in progress, possibly the laying of trolley tracks. Florence Pond Graham (1895-1975) described what occurred in 1906 when the city paved Bergen Avenue from Fairmount to Communipaw avenues with asphalt: "[Thus]…started the biggest craze that one can imagine. Everyone from 7 to 70 years of age bought roller skates and Bergen Avenue became the largest skating rink in the world…the whir of skates went on …until nearly midnight [until] some of the Bergen Avenue residents rebelled at the noise."
Courtesy of North Jersey Electric Railway Historical Society.

This same stretch of New York Avenue is pictured here as it looks today. In an effort to ease congestion, contend with growing automobile use, and provide protection for pedestrians, Jersey City's Director of Public Safety John Beggans (1865-1934) announced in January 1930 that within days all the side streets in the city would be designated with signs as one-way thoroughfares. Today Jersey City creates and maintains signage, passes and enforces traffic regulations, and cleans over 200,000 miles of streets. The number of miles was calculated by the authors of the 1910 book *Jersey City of Today*.

This is a portrait of Mary Hudspeth Benson (1824-1904), an activist in the mid-to-late nineteenth century for whom a city park is named. She was horrified at the young people being jailed and often took one home to rehabilitate rather than leave him or her with seasoned criminals who could teach the youngster more of their craft. Among her many accomplishments was to convince city officials that street cleaning could be feasible and its results beneficial. She obtained private funding and volunteers to clean the streets for six months. At the conclusion of the period, the results were so good that city-sponsored street cleaning was instituted.
Courtesy of the Jersey City Free Public Library.

This undated photo from the early twentieth century shows a team of horses pulling a water tank, which is spraying Barrow Street beside Van Vorst Park in a street-cleaning effort.
Courtesy of the Jersey City Free Public Library.

Approximately fifty years later, on November 4, 1954, an updated germicide-spraying truck is inaugurated with many folks turning out for the demonstration. It was hoped that this street-cleaning effort would "help keep our children free from the many dreaded and crippling diseases that are plaguing our country."
Dan McNulty Collection. Courtesy of the Jersey City Free Public Library.

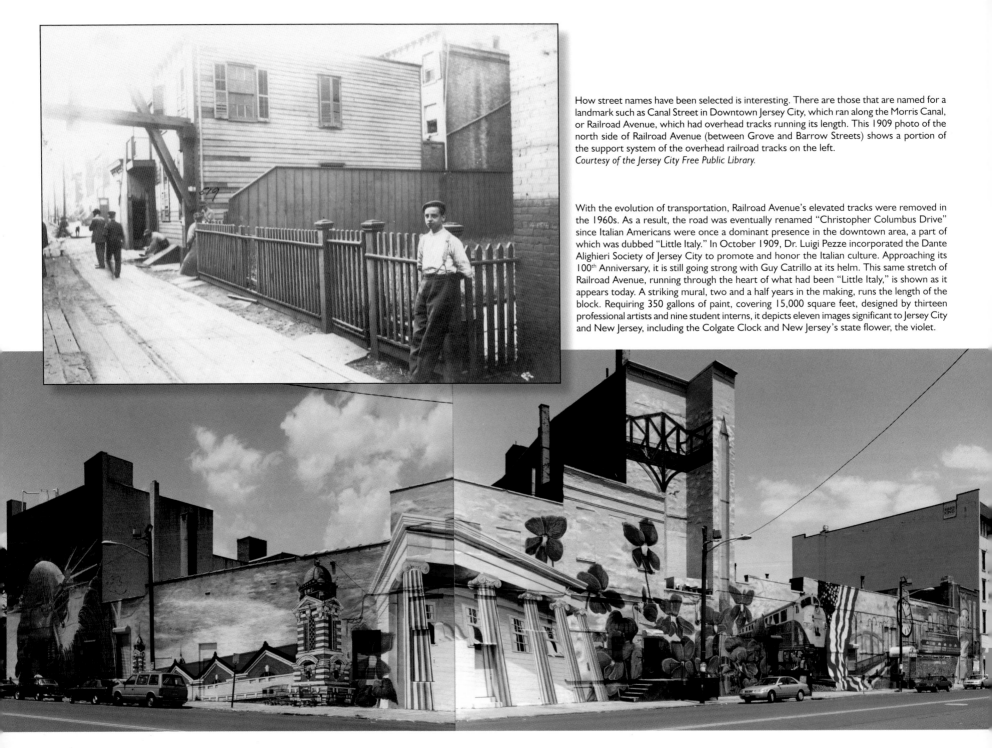

How street names have been selected is interesting. There are those that are named for a landmark such as Canal Street in Downtown Jersey City, which ran along the Morris Canal, or Railroad Avenue, which had overhead tracks running its length. This 1909 photo of the north side of Railroad Avenue (between Grove and Barrow Streets) shows a portion of the support system of the overhead railroad tracks on the left.
Courtesy of the Jersey City Free Public Library.

With the evolution of transportation, Railroad Avenue's elevated tracks were removed in the 1960s. As a result, the road was eventually renamed "Christopher Columbus Drive" since Italian Americans were once a dominant presence in the downtown area, a part of which was dubbed "Little Italy." In October 1909, Dr. Luigi Pezze incorporated the Dante Alighieri Society of Jersey City to promote and honor the Italian culture. Approaching its 100th Anniversary, it is still going strong with Guy Catrillo at its helm. This same stretch of Railroad Avenue, running through the heart of what had been "Little Italy," is shown as it appears today. A striking mural, two and a half years in the making, runs the length of the block. Requiring 350 gallons of paint, covering 15,000 square feet, designed by thirteen professional artists and nine student interns, it depicts eleven images significant to Jersey City and New Jersey, including the Colgate Clock and New Jersey's state flower, the violet.

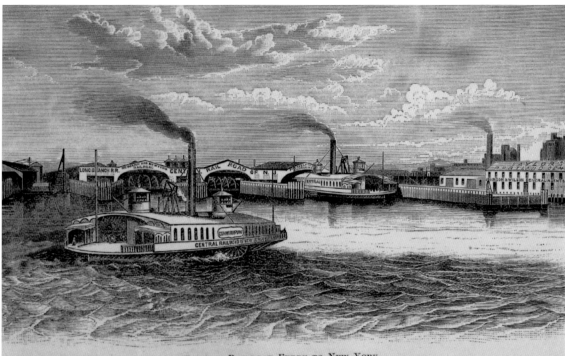

CENTRAL RAILROAD FERRY TO NEW YORK.

The ferry became the first method of mass transportation across the Hudson River. The *Communipaw Ferry* was the first legally established line in 1661. According to Charles Winfield (1874), there is no mention of it after 1672 until 1783 and again it appears to sleep until the Central Railroad of New Jersey completed its link from Elizabethport to Jersey City. Revived, it offered service from the Central Railroad Terminal in Jersey City to Liberty Street in New York. This mid-nineteenth century etching shows a ferry clearly marked *Communipaw*. In 1849, the Hudson County Board of Freeholders attempted to fix ferry fees with a list of eighty prices. The price of a child from six- to nine-years-old was 2¢; a wagon loaded with hay drawn by one horse with one rider cost 37.5¢; boxes of oranges cost more than baskets of oranges; and wagons were charged by the number of horses and/or people. This complicated method of pricing, while strongly advocated, was never enforced.
Courtesy of the Jersey City Free Public Library.

COP ARRESTS TWO TRESPASSING COWS

The Animals Have Been Spoiling Lawns and Terraces.

Patrolman De Clark of the Seventh Precinct arrested two cows yesterday afternoon for trespass. Residents in the vicinity of Sip and Tonnele avenues have made a number of complaints to the police about stray cows destroying their lawns and terraces. Stephen Zoroudes of 311 Fields Avenue was summoned to Judge Manning's court last Friday as defendant in this cow business, but he failed to appear, and has kept shady since.

A cop leading a couple of cows to the police station attracted much attention. The police notified the S. P. C. A., who sent two officers to the station house for the four legged prisoners. The owner of the cows failed to claim them.

The mode of land transportation for centuries was limited to horse and wagons, or sleighs depending upon the weather. This horse trots easily through the light snow on Clinton Avenue in front of the Jersey City Athletic Club. Horses, in their working capacity particularly, had to be protected from overloads, fallen electric lights, trolley wires, and potholes. They sometimes had to be rescued from ditches, humanely euthanized when necessary, covered with blankets in the cold, and sprayed with cooling water in the heat. The Hudson County Society for the Prevention of Cruelty to Animals oversaw such things and many others involving animals, some of which bordered on what modern society would call the bizarre. All sorts of things were reported in the daily papers including the tossing of a dead elephant off a train in Jersey City in 1914, the death of the Mercer Street Fire Engine Company #3's mascot Jimmy, a monkey, which was replaced by an alligator in 1901, and the arresting of cows as this newspaper story from 1906 reports.

71

Clockwise from top:
Mass transportation began with stagecoaches and then trolleys. This Pacific Avenue horse-drawn trolley car is from c. 1906.
Courtesy of North Jersey Electric Railway Historical Society.

By the next decade, this c. 1913 view shows the switch from horse-drawn to electric trolleys. These trolleys required the installation of tracks, but a benefit was the reduction of animal waste in the streets. Art Wilson gives a lengthy description in Chapter Six of his book, *No Experience Needed*, of the summer and winter trolley cars in Jersey City. In the summer, open-air trolley cars permitted access at any point along the running board. The winter trolleys were completely enclosed, allowing access only at the front or rear.
Courtesy of the Jersey City Free Public Library.

By the year 2000 Jersey City experienced a new "trolley." The Hudson-Bergen Light Rail opened, connecting points throughout Hudson County, and eventually Bergen County, with the Jersey City-Hoboken waterfront. It has won national recognition as a superb, efficient transportation system resulting from the partnership between the public and private sectors.

This undated c. 1940s view shows the old and the new at the Public Service Terminal (designed by John T. Rowland, Jr.) at Journal Square. Buses, trolleys, taxis, and crowds line up for the commute. The trolley car on the left headed to Jackson Avenue, a thriving business district in those days before malls. The Jackson Avenue line was the last to travel the streets of Jersey City making its final run on August 7, 1949. *Courtesy of the Jersey City Free Public Library.*

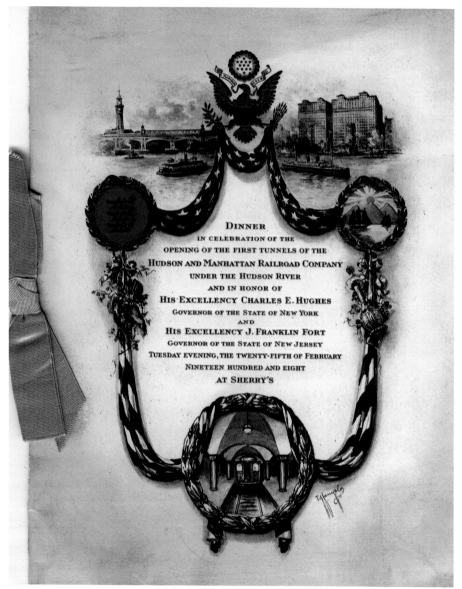

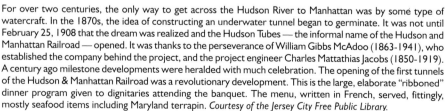

Jersey City went all out to celebrate the opening of the Tubes. There was a parade that passed through Lincoln Park (at that time called West Side Park). The marchers passed through majestic columns at the park's entrance called the *Taft Court of Honor* for then-President William Taft. The columns were only up for the occasion and were removed shortly afterwards. *Courtesy of the Jersey City Free Public Library.*

For over two centuries, the only way to get across the Hudson River to Manhattan was by some type of watercraft. In the 1870s, the idea of constructing an underwater tunnel began to germinate. It was not until February 25, 1908 that the dream was realized and the Hudson Tubes — the informal name of the Hudson and Manhattan Railroad — opened. It was thanks to the perseverance of William Gibbs McAdoo (1863-1941), who established the company behind the project, and the project engineer Charles Mattathias Jacobs (1850-1919). A century ago milestone developments were heralded with much celebration. The opening of the first tunnels of the Hudson & Manhattan Railroad was a revolutionary development. This is the large, elaborate "ribboned" dinner program given to dignitaries attending the banquet. The menu, written in French, served, fittingly, mostly seafood items including Maryland terrapin. *Courtesy of the Jersey City Free Public Library.*

Such joy existed over the opening of the tunnels that crowds gathered at several locations. This is a view of City Hall adorned with patriotic bunting and American flags as the crowd celebrates the event. Fifty-four years later, with other tunnels and modes of transportation, the Hudson and Manhattan Railroad went bankrupt. In 1962, the operation of the tunnel trains was taken over by PATH (the Port Authority Trans-Hudson Corporation).

The New Jersey Turnpike Authority was established in 1948. Between November 1951 and January 1952, a stretch of 118 miles was opened to traffic allowing easy transport from Deepwater in the south to Ridgefield in the north. In 1956, two extensions — the eight-mile section over Newark Bay and the six-mile connection to the Pennsylvania Turnpike — were opened. Mayor Bernard Berry and other dignitaries spoke with huge amplifying horns, allowing the listeners to hear every word as the city celebrated the opening of the Newark Bay-Hudson County Extension on September 15, 1956. Seated in front was the Boy Scout band with a Scout playing one of the 1950s most popular instruments, the accordion. *Dan McNulty Collection. Courtesy of the Jersey City Free Public Library.*

Many of the city streets bear the name of something geographic, whether it was the type of trees that were predominant on the street or its proximity to something. Ocean Avenue is close to the shoreline of Jersey City, indirectly close to the Atlantic Ocean. It was on this street that Dr. Peter Francis Ghee (1871-1948) lived. He was the first African-American physician in Jersey City. Educated at the Leonard Medical School in North Carolina, Ghee was licensed in New Jersey in 1898 and established his practice at 286 Fifth Street. He traveled to his patients with his faithful horse *Diane*. His grandson believes he came to Jersey City because it was the terminus for so many railroad lines and he would be able to minister to the needs of the hundreds of black Pullman Porters who worked for the railroads.

Though he was a successful doctor, he did not escape some of the prejudices of the day. When he purchased Dr. Charles Opdyke's home at 736 Ocean Avenue in 1909, such a stir was created that it was recorded in *The Jersey Journal.* The owner of the neighboring property was upset and felt that Dr. Opdyke's home was sold to a colored man to avenge a dispute between the Opdykes and himself. Mrs. Opdyke denied the allegation, but did admit, "If Mr. Klingenhoffer had treated me differently, I would have thought twice before selling my house to a colored man." Dr. Peter Ghee was an astute businessman who in later years spent much of his time with commercial concerns. Upon his death, his estate was valued at several hundred thousand dollars with interests in over one hundred properties in Jersey City. *Courtesy of Peter H. Ghee, Esq.*

Some street names are a lot more personal than those named for landmarks or national heroes. They are enduring proof of the esteem in which prominent early residents and their families were held. Each time one of those street names is uttered an early family is honored. Downtown's Varick Street was named for Colonel Richard Varick (1753-1831), a Revolutionary War hero who, along with Anthony Dey (1776-1859) and Jacob Radcliff (1764-1823), founded the Associates of Jersey Company in 1804 in the hopes of creating a city to rival New York City. The company laid the groundwork for the downtown section called "Jersey City," which would eventually become the name that encompassed all the merged sections. This portrait of Varick, by Henry Inman (1801-1846), hangs in Washington's Morristown Headquarters. *Courtesy of the Jersey City Free Public Library.*

JACOB M. MERSELES,

This particularly striking portrait is of Jacob M. Merseles (1812-1865), who was the Hudson County Sheriff. Merseles, along with Henry Newkirk (1799-1861) and John Cornelison (1802-1875), were granted, by act of the New Jersey Legislature in 1856, incorporation of the Union Omnibus Company, which gave them the right to set up stagecoach lines. His two partners also have streets named for them. Merseles was instrumental in bringing the first railroad to Jersey City in 1859. *Taylor 1857.*

Pictured is Peter Henderson (1822-1890), a gardener and florist who established a seed company. He wrote several books, including *Gardening for Profit* and *Practical Floriculture*, which are still in print today — over one hundred years after his death. For years, Henderson Street was a major thoroughfare in Jersey City. In 1982, the street name was changed to Jose Munoz Marin Boulevard for the first democratically elected Governor of Puerto Rico. *Courtesy of the Jersey City Free Public Library.*

Many of the prominent citizens of nineteenth century Jersey City had beautiful mansions. Matthew Armstrong's land included residences for himself and his son. This 1857 view of his estate on Garfield Avenue, engraved by John Orr, shows a striking home with a finely sculpted landscape. *Taylor, 1857.*

RESIDENCE OF MATTHEW ARMSTRONG, JUNIOR, BERGEN, N.J.

In this C. T. Harris photo — 150 years later — a high rise stands regally on the same block. A street sign gives mute testimony to the early days when streets were identified by the owners of the homes that graced them.

The residence of Garrett Sip (1791-1868) took up quite a plot of land along what are now Tonnelle and Sip avenues. Further east was Sip Manor, Jersey City's oldest home, which was moved to 5 Cherry Lane in Westfield, New Jersey, in 1926. With several members of the Sip family having homesteads in the area, it was only natural to name the street along which some of them lived "Sip Avenue." *Taylor, 1857.*

RESIDENCE OF GARRET SIP, BERGEN, N.J.

The next four images are of Jersey City attorney James Fleming and his Grand Street home. *Courtesy of the Jersey City Free Public Library.*

This is James Flemming (1832-1894), whose grandfather Isaac Edge (1777-1851) owned the famed Edge's Windmill built in Jersey City in 1815 on the waterfront as part of a gristmill business. James became a successful attorney who won acquittal in a second trial of Jennie Smith and Covert Bennett who were accused of murdering Jennie's husband, a Jersey City police officer. The scandalous case had garnered nation-wide attention.

One's home, then as it is now, was a place where the man was king or the woman queen. More than just a place to sleep, it provides a safe and comfortable refuge from the rest of the world. For the affluent, Jersey City offered some of the finest accommodations. This c. 1880s photo is of the interior of a home located at 80-82 Grand Street. Attorney James Flemming lived there until his 1894 death. Each room had a source of heat — this one using a pot-bellied stove in front of the fireplace. The barrister's bookcase is full and there are photographs on the walls.

The Flemming bedroom is a study in Victorian living with the intricately carved table and bed boards. Photos and pictures abound on the walls and there is, of course, the fireplace for warmth.

Perhaps this room served as a parlor in which to entertain. There are pipes and books on the table and a musical instrument on the chair. Art Wilson describes a pump organ that his family used for entertainment, "If I slackened and didn't keep a good strong, steady stroke on the pumping handle, the musical notes began to go sour and everybody groaned. Even so, I thought it was fun."

The Regina Music Box Company, begun in the early 1890s, was located at the corner of Morris and Hudson Streets. According to Alexander McLean in his 1895 book, *History of Jersey City, NJ*, it was "one of the most important manufacturing industries in Jersey City." Their business was prosperous and extended to a nation-wide clientele.

This example of a "Regina" was both a music box and grandfather clock. It was very popular since it provided music without family members having to play individual instruments. The company boasted being the first in America to make a music box "comb" (the piece of steel in which teeth had been cut and tuned to produce musical notes). They proudly had over 1,300 songs in their catalog by the second year of production.

The FAIRMOUNT HOTEL   Hudson Boulevard   Jersey City, N. J.

In keeping with an image of a hotel that is on par with its New York counterparts, the Fairmount Hotel had its doormen and porters in fashionable uniforms with the hotel initials on the collars and cap. Henry Battle (1909-1985), a hotel staff member, looks dapper in his hotel garb, ready to serve residents and visitors.
Courtesy of Bernard Harris.

If a well-to-do resident elected not to deal with the maintenance involved in home ownership, an apartment could be rented at the Fairmount Hotel at 2595 Hudson Boulevard. Completed in 1912, this "grand Lady of Jersey City" was a blend of apartments and hotel rooms meant to rival New York City's finest hotels.
Albertype Company.

The Fairmount Hotel — like so many other buildings in Jersey City — has gotten a new lease on life. During a transitional period, it was owned by Father Divine (aka George Baker, c. 1880-1965), a cult leader who considered himself God. Father Devine made it a haven for members of his Peace Center Church. After his death and the Church's membership declined, it was eventually sold to Gold Coast Realty. Forlorn and unused, it was again sold, remodeled, and opened in 1995 as a 59-unit senior citizens' residence.

81

For the average, middle-class Jersey City resident, the most practical and affordable option was a two-family home. This row of four homes at 95 to 103 Claremont Avenue is decorated for a block dance in 1917. The elderly couple on the porch of the second house is Great Grandma and Great Grandpa Fisk. *G. W. Myers, 1917.*

>

This same block of Claremont Avenue, which is between Rose Avenue and Martin Luther King Drive, was host for more than forty years to a magical light and music creation. Two neighboring families, the Kings and later the Murphys, decorated their respective homes to such a magnificent extent that it was an annual attraction for neighbors and tourists. Mary Murphy passed away in 2002, but her husband and children, in tribute to her, continued the tradition for several years thereafter.

This photo shows the block party in full swing that 1917 evening. As young Americans enlisted for service in World War I, the folks at home wanted to show their support with the goal of raising funds for the American Red Cross and selling Liberty Bonds; block parties were organized for these purposes. *G. W. Myers, 1917.*

The four homes are still standing — ninety years later. They all have upgrades to their exterior, including an enclosed porch on the second floor of the third home.

Most surviving photographs of people from the nineteenth century are posed portraits. Because of the length of exposure time necessary, subjects had to remain still. To move meant a blur. The gentleman pumping the water in this c. 1886 photo is Mungo J. Currie (1857-1923), the attorney son of John and Ellen Currie; John and Ellen owned the large farm that straddled the border between Jersey City and Bayonne. Part of the area is known, to this day, as Currie's Woods. The two children are his nieces, Helen and Jessie Imbrie, the daughters of his sister Janet Currie Imbrie. This photo was taken on farmland near what is now Pamrapo Avenue.

As the new year of 1937 started, James Meehan of Jersey City's Junior Chamber of Commerce urged interest in improving housing as "a matter of civic pride." At that time there were 30,000 dwelling structures with more than half — 15,578 — having only cold water and 15,640 with no tub or shower. Incredibly, eighty-one buildings did not have any water at all! By 1943 Jersey City had opened five public housing projects with more to follow including Currie's Woods, the remnants of which appear in the far right of this photo. The houses in the foreground are among the city's latest housing efforts. Gone are most of the high-rise projects, replaced with homey, more attractive residences that inspire pride and greatly improve Jersey City's residential landscape. *Photo by Alton O'Neill.*

Living in Jersey City meant being able to step out one's door and not go far to find that other major necessity — food. The history of the grocery store began with the public market, which evolved into the general store, and then specialty shops. As the twentieth century dawned, residents of Jersey City would shop at the butcher, the baker, the dry goods and produce stores, the fish market, and the delicatessen. This system worked well since people could purchase their needs at the particular store and carry them home in the days before the family car was a reality. Shown is the interior of the local butcher shop, the Star Market, at 465 West Side Avenue. It was run by Julius Torp, who lived in the same building. Notice the sign beside the woman advertising, "Poke Chops 5 ¢." *Courtesy of the Jersey City Free Public Library.*

With the advent of the supermarket, making a half a dozen trips just for groceries is now part of history. The Great Atlantic & Pacific Tea Company — the A & P — was the first supermarket chain in the United States. Originally a seller of tea, coffee, and spices in the nineteenth century, it evolved into the supermarket we know today. Jersey City was home to its first "no frills" A & P Economy Store opened in 1927. By the 1930s, it had added the innovation of self-service. There are three A & Ps located in Jersey City today; this one is downtown at 125-18th Street.

Eating out was becoming more popular, and what more delightful treat could there be than an ice cream sundae on a hot summer day long before air conditioning? The ice cream parlor was a very popular place and they abounded all over town for the first half of the twentieth century. Brummer's at the Junction — Communipaw Avenue and Grand Street — was one of the ice cream parlors that had the longest run. So popular was it with the teenage set that the students at Lincoln High School (located across the street from it) had a poem in their 1947 yearbook describing the benefits of Brummer's. Opened originally in the middle of the block at 737 Grand Street in 1904, it moved to its long-standing corner location at 731 Grand Street in August 1919. Founded by Frederick (1888-1950) and Catherine (1890-1987) Brummer, this c. 1926 photo shows son Fred with employees Dora Brummer Straube and Emil Mangels (1900-1974). *Courtesy of George Brummer.*

Almost ninety years after Brummer's opened on the corner of Communipaw Avenue and Grand Street, the building still stands. Purchased by Roscoe Taylor, the building has undergone a facelift and is now home to Mr. Taylor's real estate business.

Here are the Brummers' two sons, Charles (1916-1992) and Fred (1915-2002), as young boys in the ice cream parlor in the early 1920s.
Courtesey of George Brummer.

Sixty years later Charles and Fred sit on the same stools after serving generations of residents not only ice cream, but also lunches and delicious homemade chocolate. The business remained at this location for seventy years, closing in 1989. Later that year, George Brummer, grandson of Frederick and Catherine, reopened Brummer's at 125 East Broad Street in Westfield, New Jersey. No longer an ice cream parlor, it is still producing the homemade chocolates and truffles that have been part of the family tradition for over a century. In its front window are the lamps that once graced the ice cream parlor at the Junction.
Courtesy of George Brummer.

Jersey City's A List

On the subject of famous folks, Jersey City has been the birthplace of many accomplished people. Among them are actors Ozzie Nelson (1906-1975), Norma Talmadge (1893-1957), Phyllis Newman, Nathan Lane, Malcolm Jamal Warner, and Richard Conte (1910-1975). Authors Thomas Fleming and Jim Bishop (1907-1987) hail from Jersey City while Walter Dean Myers has been a resident for over three decades. Singers Marilyn McCoo, Nancy Sinatra, several members of Kool and the Gang, and opera star Astrid Varnay (1916-2005) are also Jersey City natives. Dancer Kathryn (Mrs. Arthur) Murray (1906-1999), artist Douglas Allen, composer Jerry Herman, and musician Al DiMeola also belong on this A list. The sports world is richer thanks to the likes of former Football Commissioner Paul Tagliabue, baseball player Willie Banks, and basketball players Tom Heinsohn and David Rivers. The list of remarkable people is endless; for countless numbers of Jersey City's sons and daughters have gone on to live exciting, fruitful, and dynamic lives.

This February 27, 1999 front-page article in *The Jersey Journal* tells of the naming of a portion of Kearney Avenue after one of Jersey City's favorite sons, Clerow "Flip" Wilson (1933-1998). The gifted comedian was a student at PS # 14 and produced an animated video called "Flip Wilson and the Miracle of PS 14." Flip pioneered the way for other black entertainers when, as a television personality, he developed his own variety show, "The Flip Wilson Show."
Courtesy of The Jersey Journal.

DAVID RIVERS

Basketball player David Rivers was a student at PS # 14, where his presence on a team insured its victory in the class basketball tournaments. He continued his successful career on the renowned Saint Anthony's High School basketball team under legendary coach Bob Hurley. After playing for the University of Notre Dame under Coach Digger Phelps and then the Los Angeles Lakers, David finished his professional career as a most valuable player in the European League. A man of quiet dignity and humility, David is currently CEO of his own corporation. *Courtesy of the National Basketball Association.*

One of the most prestigious and famous dance troops in the world is the Radio City Music Hall Rockettes. Created in 1925 by Jersey City born and bred Russell Markert (1899-1990), he originally called his group the Missouri Rockets since he was based in Saint Louis at the time. Discovered two years later by the owner of New York's Roxy Theater, they came east along with a name change to the Roxyettes. By 1932, they were ensconced at Radio City Music Hall as the Rockettes. Russell was their decades-long choreographer. He had seen the girls in the Ziegfeld Follies in 1922 and years later reminisced, "If I ever got a chance to get a group of American girls who would be taller and have longer legs and could really complicated tap routines and eye-high kicks…they'd knock your socks off!" He certainly succeeded! *Manhattan Postcard Company.*

PHYLLIS BARBARA NEWMAN

2350 Boulevard—C.P.

P.S. 17—Dramatic Arts

Ping Pong '47; Cheerleaders '47-'50; Public Speaking '47, '48; Order of the Lamp '49, '50; Assembly Committee '49, '50; French '46, '47; Theatre Guild '46-'48; Quill Board '50, Class Play '50.

"Did you ever see a dream walking?" Knowing Phyl, makes us say—"Why sure!" Her personality and dramatic talents are respected by all.

Author Thomas Fleming (shown) was a 1945 graduate of Saint Peter's Prep. Tom has written countless articles and over forty books including one — *Mysteries of My Father: An Irish American Memoir* — about his father Teddy Fleming's tenure as a wardsman for Mayor Frank Hague. The book presents a decades-long account of the Democratic Machine at its mightiest.

"If I had to choose one word to describe Tom Fleming as a writer, it would be master," says fellow novelist Sidney Offit.

In 2006 the Jersey City Landmarks Conservancy honored Tom with its J. Owen Grundy History Award for helping to build the community of preservation — in this case through the written word.
Courtesy of Alice Fleming.

JOSEPH A. LANE
Class Officer 1,3; Speaker's Forum 4; Dramatics 1,2,3,4; Man of the Year 4; Society of Outstanding American High School Students; Father's Club Award for Dramatics.

This is actress Phyllis Newman as she appeared in her 1950 Lincoln High School yearbook, in which she was voted "Future Hollywood Star," a prediction that truly hit the mark. (She went to PS # 17 before Lincoln.) Within two years of her graduation Phyllis debuted on Broadway in "Wish You Were Here," and in 1962, beat out Barbra Streisand for a Tony Award. Phyllis found success in music, television, and the movies, and was often a panelist on popular game shows of the 1960s including "Password" and "Truth or Consequences." She had roles on dozens of shows from "The Man from U.N.C.L.E." to "One Life to Live" to "Quincy MD," proving that those four years in the Dramatics Club of Lincoln High School were well-spent. *Lincoln High School Yearbook, June 1950.*

This is actor Nathan Lane as he appeared in his 1974 Saint Peter's Prep yearbook, *The Petrean.* Named Joseph at birth, he changed his name to Nathan after a character in "Guys and Dolls" that he played in a Dinner Theater appearance in 1978. A member of his school's Drama Club all four years, in his senior year Nathan played Teddy (Roosevelt) Brewster in "Arsenic and Old Lace." Like Phyllis, Nathan enjoyed Broadway success, winning two Tony awards, most recently for his 2001 role in "The Producers." He also went on to television and movie fame.

Fun and Games

People had to use their imaginations to create diversions and activities that were fun and engaging. The preponderance of clubs and societies was evident by the long lists in the city directories. There were clubs covering a wide range of interests. There were theaters, moving picture shows, and many traveling acts that would set up for a day or two and move on to the next venue. Sports events were popular. Art Wilson, when short the few cents to attend a game, would create a home-made grappling hook by tying rope to a horseshoe that "could be picked up in almost any vacant field and there were many of those in Greenville…before 1920." Hooking it over the fence top he then simply scrambled up the rope and over the barrier. Many activities were homegrown, using a minimum of materials and a maximum of ingenuity. Take a look at how people have had fun over the years.

Two common sights on Jersey City's streets were the ponies to ride and the organ grinder and his monkey.
According to Florence Pond Graham, c. 1905 the organ grinder played while "the monkey would jump on our shoulders and tip his little red cap when we gave him a few pennies."
The pony was a popular prop for the roving photographer during the first half of the twentieth century. The pure delight on two-year-old Everett Donaldson's face says it all in this c. 1953 photo taken downtown on Mercer Street. *Courtesy of Bernard Harris.*

Art Wilson describes Halloween as a time to draw with colorful chalk all over town and fill socks with chalk with which to mark each other. Halloween "was not with costumes and the 'trick-or-treat' routine we know today. That kind of door-to-door begging in outlandish garments was done on Thanksgiving Day." By Halloween 1957 the custom had become what we know today. Here the crowd of onlookers in the bleachers is enjoying the procession of youngsters as they show off their Halloween costumes in a parade around Audubon Park. *Dan McNulty Collection. Courtesy of the Jersey City Free Public Library.*

Both Florence and Art describe the clothing of their times including the fact that boys did not wear long pants until they were in their teens. Art even has a chapter in his book, "Farewell to Knickers: Age 14 – 1923." A decade later, we see that the practice of little boys wearing knee-length pants with stockings, which had been the standard, was no longer being strictly adhered to. These adorable little girls and several dapper little boys in top hats participated in the May Walk in Lincoln Park in 1933. *Courtesy of Daryl Delgaizo Levy.*

There are dozens of parks offering a green retreat from the hustle and bustle of Jersey City. Many of the parks are named for people of Jersey City who were instrumental in making life a little better for all of us. This little park tucked in the Lafayette section is named for a physician who practiced a few blocks away on Pacific Avenue. Dr. Lena Edwards (1900-1986) was one of the first African American women doctors to practice in Jersey City, serving the needs of many immigrant women. During her retirement, she went to Texas where she worked to get a small mission hospital built for migrant workers.
Photo by C. T. Harris.

The parks of Jersey City remain a haven for fun and excitement as this c. 2002 Alton O'Neill photo, taken at Hamilton Park, indicates.

This July 17, 1947 photo was taken at Goodman's Furniture Store on Bergen Avenue. Television was in its infancy. To see this marvel in action was a great treat, so people swarmed to Goodman's for the opportunity. The tiny screen is barely visible as a little white rectangle in the rear of this photo.
Dan McNulty Collection. Courtesy of Jersey City Free Public Library.

The largest circuses in the nineteenth century performed in Jersey City. In the second week of *The Jersey Journal's* existence, Forepaugh's Circus and Menagerie's visit was advertised. Adam Forepaugh (1831-1890) sold half his acts to the Bailey circus and his train cars to Ringling Bros.
"The Greatest Show on Earth" — the Ringling Brothers and Barnum & Bailey Circus — was heralded days before in *The Jersey Journal* with photos and descriptions including that the circus would arrive in four trains of 100 double-length, solid-steel railroad cars hauling 1,600 people, seven herds of elephants, seven hundred horses, and 1,009 menagerie animals. It was set up in Washington Park in the Heights. Coming from a two-day gig in Newark, two performances were held June 12, 1935 before the circus continued on its way to Paterson. This photo shows Arthur Wright and His Side Show Band, an all-black ensemble that the Ringling Brothers employed until 1948.

Dances were frequent social events for many organizations. For much of the early twentieth century, it was customary for a young lady to have a dance card. It had a duel purpose: to list the scheduled dances along with a line for a young man to sign on as the lady's dance partner and also to be kept as a memento of the evening. This was the card used by the ladies attending the Bayview Craftsmen's Club Dinner Dance on January 22, 1927. The dinner included filet mignon and among the artists performing was the Jersey City Police Quartet.

This exuberant crowd was assembled in the Stanley Theater at Journal Square on a Saturday in February 1950. The theater, which opened in 1928, looks like it had all 4,300 seats filled. As Florence Pond Graham recalled, attendance at opening night was by invitation only and Mayor Frank Hague (1875-1956) took to the stage to welcome the new venture. For sixty years, it hosted some of the biggest entertainers of the times as well as blockbuster movies. The large number of children in the audience may be explained by the fact that Porky Pig was at Journal Square that day.
Dan McNulty Collection. Courtesy of the Jersey City Free Public Library.

The 1921 Dempsey-Carpentier fight may be Jersey City's most famous, but outdoor boxing matches were a common form of entertainment with sparring matches sometimes held at Journal Square to stir interest before the actual fight. This boxing match was held at Paulus Hook Park at the corner of Washington and Grand streets July 8, 1959. This amateur boxing show was sponsored by the Jersey City Department of Parks. All nine bouts were no decisions.
Dan McNulty Collection. Courtesy of the Jersey City Free Public Library.

One of the focal points in Jersey City, where much entertainment as well as serious business took place, was the Fourth Regiment Armory. Originally located on Bergen Avenue, where the Tuers farm stood and now Hudson Catholic High School stands, it was erected in 1895. It burned down in June 1927. The massive structure with its lookout towers and iron grill work made fighting the fire one of Jersey City Fire Department's greatest challenges. Here, with plans for the current Armory's facelift, Mayor Glenn Cunningham holds a photo of the original Armory, as Department of Recreation director, Bob Hurley, looks on. *Photo by Alton O'Neill.*

In its 32-year history, the Armory hosted countless events and exhibitions. This photo shows the entrance to the Municipal Exhibit held there in 1913. The theme of the show was "Know Your City." Many aspects of city life were represented from the Shade Tree Commission's accomplishments to a replica of the Peter Stuyvesant statue at Bergen Square. The arch under which the people are entering was saved after the fire and placed in Pershing Field, as seen in this recent photo.

The presentation by the Department of Health offered recommendations such as "Don't patronize milk dealers who fill their bottles on the streets. Insist on having your supply of milk filled on the farm and by a sanitary filler." It offered information on infectious diseases and flies. The exhibit advised on the proper use of refuse cans and iceboxes. In short, it presented a plethora of information designed to educate people how to keep themselves and their families healthy.

In an effort to improve their exhibit from the previous year, the Jersey City Police Department developed a presentation that featured a miniature police headquarters that included a beautiful, massive station house desk manned by a uniformed officer. Various tools of the trade, including the relatively new candlestick telephone, were displayed. Very striking was the large sculpture of a policeman assisting a child.

The Jersey City Fire Department showed many photos of the equipment and firemen in action. Also exhibited was the first motor driven steam engine that the city had just purchased that year along with a life-saving net.

In 1935, the Fourth Regiment Armory was replaced by the New Jersey National Guard Armory. Designed by architect Hugh A. Kelly (1888-1966), it was constructed on Montgomery Street just a block east of the original Armory location. It held sporting events — including boxing matches in which Sonny Liston defeated Chuck Wepner and Jersey City Mayor Thomas F. X. Smith (1927-1996) "fought" Mohammad Ali — and, as with its predecessor, it hosted all kinds of exhibits such as the *Hudson County Progress Exposition* and the *Home Beautiful Exposition*. This is a scene on opening day of the *International Auto Show* held at the Armory January 12-16, 1955. Perfume was to be given to the first five hundred women to attend and proceeds of the show benefited the Jersey City Community Fund.
Dan McNulty Collection. Courtesy of the Jersey City Free Public Library.

The Main Library has been a destination for adventure for over a century. Dr. Leonard Gordon (1844-1905), then-President of the Board of Trustees, had worked tirelessly to see the project through — from the acquisition of the land in 1896 to the opening of its doors on January 16, 1901. Hours were, at one time, long, with Sundays until 10 p.m. being the standard. As our culture has evolved so has the Library. It now offers Internet service, workshops on a wide array of topics, cultural programs, summer reading programs for children, and talks by varied and esteemed personalities. Eleven branch locations and a bookmobile service residents in all parts of the city.
Courtesy of the Jersey City Free Public Library.

Jersey City unveiled its first traveling library, the Bookmobile, on March 15, 1954. This new "branch" brings the total number of locations for the Library to a lucky thirteen. It provides access to books to families, the disabled, and senior citizens right in their own neighborhoods.
Dan McNulty Collection. Courtesy of the Jersey City Free Public Library.

On May 8, 2008 a state-of-the-art Bookmobile became the library's latest acquisition. It is ADA compliant with a lift allowing easy access for persons in wheelchairs. The Bookmobile has Internet capability and follows two alternating routes. It is the latest achievement of Library director, Priscilla Gardner (inset). During her tenure, which began in 2001, the Library has seen the metamorphosis of the small neighborhood Claremont Branch into a large regional library, the Glenn D. Cunningham Library, named in honor of Jersey City's first African American mayor. The long-awaited demolition and rebuilding of the book storage building, "the Stacks," is underway, and an overhaul of the Greenville Regional Branch, the establishment of computer training classes, Dial-a-Story for children, and many other innovations have taken place in the dawn of this new century. *Photo by C. T. Harris.*

Americans love to celebrate. They choose a variety of ways, but one of the most enduring has been the parade. When John Adams wrote to his wife Abigail about that fateful day in July of 1776, he said, "It ought to be commemorated as the day of deliverance…to be solemnized with pomp and parade, with shows, games, sports, guns, bells, bonfires…from one end of this continent to the other, from this time forward forevermore." Jersey City heeded that call, as it has found a multitude of reasons to have parades.

Decoration Day, the original name given to Memorial Day, was a time to honor those who had given their lives — the ultimate gift — to their country while in the military armed forces. The Armory figured prominently in the background of this view of the 1909 Decoration Day Parade. Heralded by *The Jersey Journal* as the "Biggest Event in the City's History," there were over 12,000 marchers including two future governors — Edward I. Edwards (1863-1931) and A. Harry Moore (1879-1952), then-Governor John Fort (1852-1920), veterans, and many other groups from the Jersey City Grocers Association to the New York Letter Carriers. At the reviewing stand children from several Jersey City orphanages were assembled and 1,500 schoolgirls dressed in red, white, and blue formed a living flag when viewed from the distance. Here, a wagon drawn by two horses decked out in American flags passes the main entrance.
Courtesy of the Jersey City Free Public Library.

When the troops returned from the First World War, the WELCOME HOME was tremendous. As the doughboys came marching home through the streets of Jersey City on May 20, 1919, they were wholeheartedly and ardently cheered on. The white-clad ladies of the Brunswick Laundry Singing Society were among the many groups represented this day. *The Jersey Journal* described the day as the "Biggest Ovation in [the] City's History" where the city "could only shout wild inarticulate things that throbbed with mad joy, with reverberating pride, with passionate love. A whole city's heart was stripped bear and laid, warm and pulsing, at the feet of those who had come home from a holy war for humanity." *Courtesy of the New Jersey State Archives, Department of State.*

Originally Paulus Hook was a small island separated from Harsimus by a marsh. During the Revolutionary War, after the American defeat at the Battle of Long Island in August 1776, the fort at Paulus Hook was abandoned since British occupation was imminent. American Major Henry "Light Horse Harry" Lee (1756-1818) launched a daring attack in 1779. While not successful, its gutsy attempt to regain the fort boosted morale tremendously. This view shows the crowd that gathered 124 years later in 1903 as a monument was dedicated in remembrance of the battle. *Courtesy of the Jersey City Free Public Library.*

These Civil War veterans gathered on the steps of the newly constructed Margaret Hague Maternity Hospital in the early 1930s. They were members of the C. Van Houten Post of GAR, the Grand Army of the Republic. Colonel Patrick Tumulty (1848-1934) — the last person on the far right in the front row — entered the 21st New Jersey Infantry at age fifteen to fight in the Civil War. Though he fought in many Native American battles and was present when Custer's nemesis Sitting Bull surrendered, he always felt that the Native Americans were exploited by the white man. His nephew, Joseph Patrick Tumulty (1879-1954), a veteran of the Spanish American War, was personal secretary to President Woodrow Wilson. *Courtesy of the Jersey City Free Public Library.*

Troops were called out for many reasons besides war. By order of President Ulysses Grant, troops were dispatched to South Carolina October 18, 1876, to oversee the November election. Bitter feelings between Republicans and Democrats over the former's Reconstruction policies resulted in riots across the state including the infamous Hamburg Massacre. This group is departing from Jersey City as reported in the November 11, 1876 edition of *Frank Leslie's Illustrated Newspaper.*

World War II saw continued high patriotism. There were war bond drives to raise funds to finance the war. Journal Square was a prominent location for such events. During the drive in 1945, a gleaming and luxurious Mercedes Benz was displayed; the 20th Armored Division had captured it from the German Army. That the enemy should be motoring about in a lavish vehicle while a countless number of their countrymen were suffering and dying made an impact. Also displayed during the war bond drive was a submarine that had been captured from the Japanese.
Courtesy of the Jersey City Free Public Library.

Traditions to honor our war dead are varied. A park on Palisade Avenue is named in honor of Sergeant Joseph Anthony (1924-1945), a Dickinson High School baseball star who was recruited by the Dodgers and Giants. However, patriotism was high and Joseph, following in the footsteps of his two older brothers, joined the service. He flew thirty-nine missions, but was killed in action. He was awarded the Flying Heart, and on May 1, 1949 this park was named in his honor. It held special significance since it was where Sergeant Anthony honed his baseball skills. Growing up, he lived directly across the street at 87 Palisade Avenue. This photo shows a Memorial Day celebration in which a heart-shaped wreath was placed in the park and a Proclamation from the city presented by then Mayor Glenn Cunningham. The Mayor and his wife, Sandra Bolden Cunningham, are behind the assembled group. Barbara Petrick, Ph.D., a retired Dickinson High School teacher as well as author and researcher of Jersey City history, stands beside the portrait of Sergeant Anthony.
Photo by Alton O'Neill.

Sadly, as time goes on, we find ourselves engaged in new wars. This simple but striking mural was painted on the side of PS # 5 by Board of Education employee Paul Marlu Maiellaro and pals Andrew Guzzi (1931-2007) and Anthony Cioffi (1930-2004). As 13-year-olds on V-J Day, August 14, 1945, they painted the World War II portion of the mural amid the gaiety and rejoicing of a block party complete with victrola and dancing. As time passed, memorials for Korea and Vietnam were added. To this day, Paul periodically refreshes the paint and keeps the message of acknowledgment and gratitude alive.

On February 26, 2003 a section of Bay Street, where Newark and Erie streets intersect, was named Joseph Lovero Way after a dispatcher working for the Jersey City Fire Department. A trained EMT, Joseph rushed to the World Trade Center to assist after the terrorist attacks on 9/11 and was killed as the Twin Towers collapsed.
Photo by Alton O'Neill.

As the United States currently struggles with the war in Iraq, we express gratitude to the new generation of soldiers who continue to fight the battles. At City Hall, a Welcome the Troops Rally c. 2003 was held to show support for our brave young men and women.
Photo by Alton O'Neill.

Brave warriors are but one reason to have a parade. Jersey City finds many reasons to celebrate. Archimedes Giacomantonio (1906-1988) designed a statue of Christopher Columbus that was erected in Journal Square in time for the 1950 Columbus Day Parade. Four days earlier, the Hudson County Freeholders had approved naming the Kennedy Boulevard Bridge, over the railroad tracks a block north of Journal Square, in the explorer's honor. The statue and bridge dedication were held on the day of the parade, October 15. This was a segment of the parade as it passed through Journal Square. The first of the three floats was for the Jersey City Football Giants; the second hauled a replica of one of Christopher Columbus' ships; and the third was sponsored by *The Jersey Journal*.
Dan McNulty Collection. Courtesy of the Jersey City Free Public Library.

The Shriners of North America is a Masonic organization that supports twenty-two hospitals for children. Hudson County's Shrine Club sponsored a parade on October 20, 1951 as part of the celebration of the induction of two hundred new members into the Salaam Temple. Contingents of Shriners from Hudson, Bergen, Essex, Union, and Passaic counties marched from the Armory to the Boulevard, to Journal Square, and finally past the reviewing stand at Bergen Square.
Courtesy of the Jersey City Free Public Library.

The next four images showcasing various parades in Jersey City were taken by photographer Alton O'Neill.

Jersey City's various organizations embrace and celebrate all the groups that strive to make a difference. The North Jersey Navigators is a Wheelchair Sports USA team started by A. Harry Moore teacher Pat Putt (1944-2001) in 1983. Focusing on track and field events for disabled students, it has participated in the Dominican and Puerto Rican parades in Jersey City. The team is shown here in a recent parade marching down Montgomery Street with the Armory in the rear.

Parades provide a particularly fun way to demonstrate pride in our diverse heritages. The participants in the Caribbean Parade show off incredibly vibrant and colorful costumes as they march past City Hall along Montgomery Street. A summertime extravaganza, this parade was held July 27, 2002.

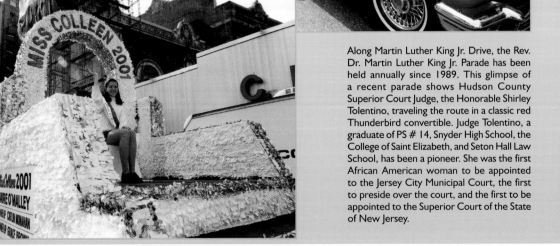

Saint Patrick's Day has been splendidly celebrated in Jersey City for well over a century. The city's Irish population surged with their immigration in the 1840s. By the 1860s, Jersey City was celebrating Saint Patrick with an annual parade. This float is carrying the 2001 Miss Colleen as it passes through Journal Square. Barely visible behind the arch on the float is the scaffolded tower of Loew's Theater as renovations were proceeding.

Along Martin Luther King Jr. Drive, the Rev. Dr. Martin Luther King Jr. Parade has been held annually since 1989. This glimpse of a recent parade shows Hudson County Superior Court Judge, the Honorable Shirley Tolentino, traveling the route in a classic red Thunderbird convertible. Judge Tolentino, a graduate of PS # 14, Snyder High School, the College of Saint Elizabeth, and Seton Hall Law School, has been a pioneer. She was the first African American woman to be appointed to the Jersey City Municipal Court, the first to preside over the court, and the first to be appointed to the Superior Court of the State of New Jersey.

Chapter Five:

Educating & Governing

Public Schools

Educated in Jersey City at Saint Peter's Prep and College, Will Durant, along with his wife Ariel, author of the multi-volume classic twentieth century masterpiece *The History of Civilization*, said, "Education is the transmission of civilization." And indeed it is. The Dutch founded Jersey City in 1660 and, fully understanding the concept expressed by Will Durant, wasted little time in establishing a school for the children of their young settlement. Administered by the Dutch Reformed Church for over one hundred years, Engelbert Steenhuysen became the first licensed schoolmaster in what would someday become New Jersey on October 6, 1662. An area was selected in the heart of Bergen Square where the original school was located. Upon that spot, for the last three and a half centuries, a school has continually been in service. Originally, possibly in the schoolmaster's residence or a church building, a stone structure was erected in 1708. Demolished near the end of the century, the third known structure, the Columbia Academy, was erected in 1790.

As the nineteenth century dawned, a convoluted series of steps resulted in the eventual merger of the various sections — Paulus Hook, Harsimus, Van Vorst, Jersey City, Bergen, Lafayette, Hudson City, and Greenville. In 1873, with the final addition of Greenville, Jersey City's boundaries became what they are today. There were schools in all the sections, which came under the aegis of the newly formed Board of Education. Throughout the mergers, secessions, and rejoinings, the school site at Bergen Square never faltered but continued its progress, with new buildings constructed in 1857, 1903, and 1966.

As the value of education became more accepted, the public system in Jersey City could not adequately provide instruction for all the children who wished to attend. Through the end of the nineteenth century, hundreds, sometimes several thousand, children were turned away from the schools since there simply was not enough room. When Mark Fagan ran for Mayor in the early twentieth century, one of his campaign promises was "A Seat for Every Child." While there was finally room for all children, overcrowding continued to be a problem. As late as the 1970s some schools still operated on the "Copenhagen" schedule in which two classes shared one classroom with each class getting four hours of instruction a day: 8:30-12:30 and 12:30-4:30.

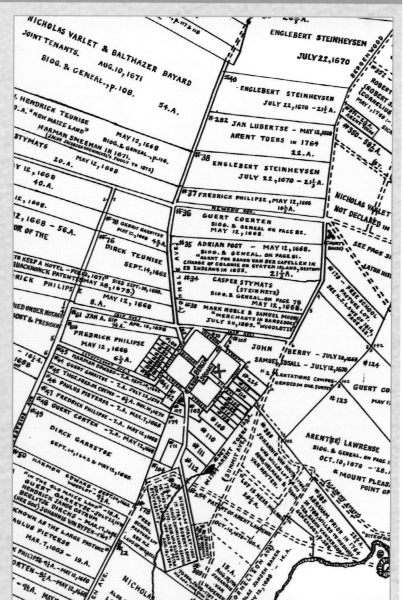

In 1660, Jacques Cortelyou (c. 1625-1693) surveyed the land and marked the lines of the central square and four surrounding blocks that would be fortified. This map was compiled and drawn from *Winfield's History of Land Titles of Hudson County, NJ 1609-1871* by D. Stanton Hammond, J.D. (1887-1982) for the Genealogical Society of New Jersey. To this day, the square remains on the same footprint developed almost 350 years ago. *Bergen Town and Township Map, Genealogical Society of New Jersey.*

COLUMBIAN ACADEMY
(From an Old Print.)

The Legislature of Bergen passed an act creating the Board of Education, which held its first meeting January 14, 1852. At this time the school trustees were appointed; taxation allowed a superintendent of schools to be selected. The curriculum was limited to spelling, reading, arithmetic, grammar, geography, and bookkeeping. When this building was constructed in 1857, some of the stones from the Columbia Academy were embedded in the rear wall of the new building. In the next decade, this building became PS # 11. By 1868 Bergen had four public schools and one colored school in the basement of the African Methodist Church on Rock Street near Academy Street. *Courtesy of the Jersey City Free Public Library.*

The earliest school was administered by the Dutch Reformed Church, but images of the first two schoolhouses to sit on Bergen Square are lost to us. In 1763, an Act of Incorporation was obtained, creating the Bergen Columbia Academy with a seven-member Board of Trustees. It is known that the second building was built in 1708 and used until 1790 when the Columbia Academy, shown here, was finally erected. This etching was done by John William Orr (1815-1887). Teachers did not spare the rod and various forms of physical punishment were employed including requiring the culprit to stand with arms at ninety-degree angles holding books, the weight of which was determined by the severity of the offense. By 1829 the Columbia Academy was charging quarterly; the fee was 25¢ for alphabet, 50¢ for spelling and writing, 75¢ for all of the above plus arithmetic. Another quarter added geography to the list. *Winfield, 1874.*

During the week of October 15-23, 1910, Jersey City celebrated the 250th Anniversary of the establishment of Bergen, Jersey City's original name given by the Dutch. Schools were closed for two and a half days and celebration was paramount. On October 24th the children from PS # 11 presented tableaux commemorating events in the city's early history. Fittingly, the exercises were held at Bergen Square with 15,000 persons in attendance. And, of course, there was a parade. This Real Photo Postcard features a float showing the pioneers of the first school. Then, as floats often do now, it had a local general contractor's name along the bottom as a sponsor.

With the consolidation of Bergen, old Jersey City, and Hudson City in 1870, followed by the addition of Greenville in 1873, the school system reflected the Jersey City as we know it today. By 1902 the local papers were reporting about the dire condition of PS # 11. The ceiling in classes four and five "fell with a crash while the classes were in session, but, fortunately, the little ones escaped injury." Additionally, a building had been annexed on Tuers Avenue. In 1903, under the aegis of architect John T. Rowland, Jr. (1871-1945), a new building was planned after additional land was purchased on the north and east sides. On February 1, 1905 the new PS # 11 opened with twenty-six classrooms and seats for 1,446 students. This 1910 Real Photo Postcard shows the school decorated for the 250th Anniversary Celebration of the establishment of Bergen.

On October 3, 1966, disaster struck when PS # 11 burned beyond repair. It was determined that four teenage boys broke into the school and one tossed some books onto an electric range. Howard Associates of New York designed the newest PS # 11, which replaced the fifth school on that site. Almost a year to the day after Dr. Martin Luther King, Jr.'s assassination, PS # 11 was named in honor of the Civil Rights leader.

The first PS # 9 was a primary school on Tonnelle Avenue near Saint Paul's Avenue. A small, sub-standard building, it was abandoned in the early 1890s. On July 8, 1895 ground was broken for one of the most magnificent school buildings of the nineteenth century. A new school at a new location — Brunswick, Wayne, and Mercer streets — PS # 9 opened in September 1896 to much fanfare, presided over by Mayor Peter Wanser (1849-1918). It was designed by architect Rudolph W. Sailer (c. 1863-1947).
Courtesy of the Jersey City Free Public Library.

This is the seventh grade classroom of Miss Julia Harney (1876-1960) who went on to become an important leader in the school system. She received her Ph.D. in 1931 from New York University with a thesis entitled, *The Evolution of Public Education in Jersey City,* which is still referenced by scholars today. This beautiful school was headed by Principal Joseph H. Brensinger (1846-1924) who also played a significant role in the development of the school system. PS # 17 is named in his honor.
Courtesy of the Jersey City Free Public Library.

SCHOOL No 14

Around the time when the sections were merging, there was a rush to create schools. Each section had four or five schools, but, as they all came together, school number names had to be changed and more schools established. In 1869, PS # 14, designed by architect John Remsen Onderdonk (1840-1888), opened its doors. This delightful little school, situated on Union Street between Jackson Avenue and Sackett Street, even had the traditional tower with a school bell to summon the children to class. Shown in this Real Photo Postcard, it became overcrowded quickly, as did all the schools of the era, and the cornerstone was laid for a second PS # 14 on May 6, 1908 to the cheers of a crowd of 4,000. Four students who had entered the original PS # 14 in 1869 were in attendance. Designed by architect John T. Rowland, Jr., it opened the following year. The two school buildings operated simultaneously with one serving the primary population, the other the grammar students. In 1953, they were both demolished and the present PS # 14 erected.

Built in 1953 and designed by Christian H. Ziegler (1881-1957), the third PS # 14 stands at 153 Union Street. A three-story annex, designed by Richard B. Rivardo, Jr. and housing eleven classrooms, was added to the east end of the school in 1973. *Photo by C. T. Harris.*

This classroom scene in PS # 14 took place April 13, 1949. It would be another four years before this eighty-year-old classroom held little ones for the last time.
Dan McNulty Collection. Courtesy of the Jersey City Free Public Library.

Hired by the Board of Education in 1865, Abner D. Joslin (1837-1932) served as the first principal of PS # 14 from 1869 to 1872. He was then transferred to PS # 12, where he was principal for most of the next forty-one years, retiring at the end of 1913. Several hundred people attended his retirement party including Governor-elect James Fielder (1867-1954), who had been one of his students. Principal Joslin was gifted with steamship tickets to Panama for a well-earned vacation and then retired to Oxford, Massachusetts, where his niece Ada and nephew Dr. Elliott Joslin, a pioneer in diabetes research, lived. *Courtesy of the Jersey City Free Public Library.*

In the fall of 1987, Ollie E. Culbreth, Jr. (1939-1995) took the helm as principal of PS # 14. Interestingly, he was in the last class to graduate from the old buildings in 1953. He retired in 1990 from the school he had started in as a student in the 1940s. Tragically, he died in an automobile accident in 1995. His long and touching association with PS # 14 was culminated in the naming of the school in 1998 for him. The headline in *The Jersey Journal* read, "To Sir, with lots of love for a class act." *Courtesy of Rev. Dr. Ada Culbreth.*

JOHN T. ROWLAND, Jr.

John T. Rowland, Jr. was a man of incredible vision and creativity. This prolific architect designed all four of the public high schools — Dickinson, Lincoln, Ferris, and Snyder, over twenty elementary schools, seven parochial schools, and the A. Harry Moore School. His work was by no means limited to just schools. He planned all but two of the buildings of the Medical Center complex and Frank Hague's Jersey City home at 2600 Kennedy Boulevard. Journal Square has the Rowland touch with the *Jersey Journal* Building, the Labor Bank, the southern wing of the former Trust Company Bank, and the Public Service Building — they are all testimony to his incredible skill. Respectful and informative caricatures of prominent citizens such as this one were popular in the first few decades of the twentieth century. *Courtesy of the Jersey City Free Public Library.*

In October 1917, newly elected Mayor Frank Hague presided over the installation of two cornerstones: one for a new Board of Education Building at 2 Harrison Avenue; the other, for a new PS # 4. This photo is of one of those events. PS # 4 was the school that Mayor Hague had attended. Thus, with hundreds of children in attendance, he spoke of the guidance he received from "Old Man" Kelley (Principal Edward Kelley), stating, "Right here I received the training that fitted me to go out into the strife of the world and I feel that had I went to any other school, I would not have received so good an education." He did not graduate, but that was not uncommon for the times. In November 1951, the Board of Education passed a resolution approving the leasing of PS # 4 to Pastor Leo P. Hak (1903-1960) of Saint Anthony of Padua Church. Shortly thereafter, the church re-christened PS # 4 as Saint Anthony's High School. *Courtesy of the Jersey City Free Public Library.*

Through the end of the nineteenth century and well into the twentieth, the Board of Education was constantly scrambling to provide sufficient classroom space for the city's burgeoning population. In January of 1901, it was reported in the papers that the city had purchased the lots from the estate of William Ogden upon which a new school for the Heights would be built. That school, PS # 28, was designed by John T. Rowland, Jr. This is the site, located on Hancock Avenue between South and Bowers Streets, in its preliminary stage of excavation by Kenny & Son Contractors. *Courtesy of the Jersey City Free Public Library.*

Public School No. 28. Jersey City, N. J.

Published by Voigt & Staeb, Jersey City N. J. (Germany). No. 14

On October 22, 1901, the cornerstone for the new Heights school, PS # 28, was laid with Mayor Edward Hoos (1850-1912) officiating. The school opened the following September. A Mrs. Heath sent this postcard to a gentleman in Millburn, New Jersey in 1906, stating, "[This is] the school where my niece teaches."
Voigt & Staeb Post Card Company.

By the early 1980s, the original PS # 28 was in poor condition. The building of a new one in a developed neighborhood presented a host of problems. The city had to condemn and demolish twenty-two homes. Mary Yockel (1927-1998) owned the home at 164 Cambridge Avenue; it was customized with so much equipment designed for the handicapped — Mary and her husband Joseph (1930-1980) — that it was more economical for the Board of Education to move the home to a lot across the street at 173 Cambridge Avenue rather than duplicate the special construction. The home was moved in December 1986; ground was broken in April 1988; and the school (shown here in 2008) opened in September 1990.

The flush of victory on this young relay race winner's face says it all. Sixth grader Walter Ramsey (1917-1993) was representing PS # 6 on June 7, 1929. The JWW initials on his shirt stand for Jotham W. Wakeman (1839-1922), who was principal of PS # 6 for an incredible fifty-seven years. He was at his desk working for the last time on the Monday before Thanksgiving of 1921 and died two months later at age 81. Principal Wakeman left such an indelible mark on the school he helped mold that Mayor Hague instigated the naming of PS # 6 in his honor. The Board of Education officially made the name change on February 1, 1928 making PS # 6 the first elementary school in the city to be named for a person. *Courtesy of the Jersey City Free Public Library.*

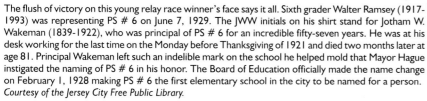

General Joseph Brensinger had been the principal of PS # 3, then PS # 9, and finally the Teachers' Training School when it was relocated to the new PS # 9 in 1896. The Training School was later moved to PS # 17 at which time Gen. Brensinger was also moved and entrusted with the principalship of both the Training School and PS # 17. A Civil War veteran, Brensinger reached the rank of General by brevet upon retirement from the Fourth Regiment National Guard. He organized the Fife and Drum Cadet Corps at PS # 17, which performed at many school and city functions. Members of the Corps assembled in front of the school each morning to raise the flag on the flagpole and returned at the end of day to lower it. The Corps became prominent locally and was a staple in parades, cornerstone celebrations, and other important city functions. PS # 17 was named in Principal Brensinger's honor on December 9, 1947. *Courtesy of the Jersey City Free Public Library*

GRADUATING CLASS OF JUNE '96.
JERSEY CITY HIGH SCHOOL.

Board of Education meeting minutes show members broached the subject of adding a high school to the school system in 1868 and each year thereafter. Finally, on October 31, 1872, the high school opened on the uppermost floor of PS # 5, the construction of which had only been completed the year before. On the evening of December 23 the building was destroyed by fire. Classes resumed in the Kepler Market building until PS # 5 was rebuilt in December 1873. Applicants for admission had to pass a test and the first few years saw an average of a quarter of the applicants rejected. This photo features members of the June 1896 class. Graduation ceremonies were held in the Academy of Music. Since girls went to high school as part of their preparation for teaching, they were the majority in the early classes. *Courtesy of the Jersey City Free Public Library.*

An 1895 Jersey City High School autograph book was sold a couple years back on eBay. Then, as now, students wrote messages — some silly, some sentimental, and some short — to their friends. This page is one from a little orange velvet covered album that appears to have belonged to 1895 graduate Caroline Bishop. Touchingly, her granddaughter wrote a message to her on the last page sixty-five years later in 1960.

In addition to academics, girls were trained in the home arts with cooking and sewing classes such as this one at Dickinson High School c. 1920s. Boys were steered to the industrial arts with an impressive slate of classes offered. In the mid-1970s, after the passage in 1972 of Title 9, the Equal Opportunity in Education Act, Jersey City's Public Schools routinely offered girls and boys the opportunity to take classes in either category. *Courtesy of the Jersey City Free Public Library.*

During July and August of 1918, with World War I still raging, Dickinson High School was partially transformed into a Trade Training Detachment of the United States Army. The school already had magnificent industrial shops offering training in such subjects as building, carpentry, electricity, and running a foundry. The expanse of property surrounding the school provided ample space for outdoor training. This view shows the work of two competing classes in the construction of the framing for two buildings as part of the Army Training Detachment. *Courtesy of Barbara Petrick.*

The curriculum and course work were demanding and the staff of the two high schools, Dickinson and Lincoln, held sterling credentials from the major Ivy League Schools including Columbia, Yale, Harvard, and Cornell. By the 1920s boys had evened out the playing field, making up roughly half the enrollment. However, there was definitely a steering toward specific subjects based upon sex. This Geometry class at Dickinson High School is predominantly male with only two girls apparent in the photo. *Courtesy of the Jersey City Free Public Library.*

Private Schools

The public school system was not the only means of educating the people. During this time of growth and struggle, Jersey City was significantly aided by many private schools offering education to thousands of children. Initially, such schools were run by individuals in private homes such as Miss Eliza Wardell at 221 Sherman Avenue in the Heights or the Misses Capron at 80 Ocean Avenue in Greenville. Often boys fared better than girls with actual school buildings devoted to their education such as the Lyceum Classical School for Boys on Grand Street, founded in 1839 by William L. Dickinson (1839-1883), the eventual Superintendent of Schools in Jersey City for whom the first public high school in Jersey City was named. The largest provider of private education in the twentieth century was the Roman Catholic Church. At its zenith in the 1960s, there were twenty-six grammar schools and eight high schools. A very small number of other Christian and Jewish schools operated at the time.

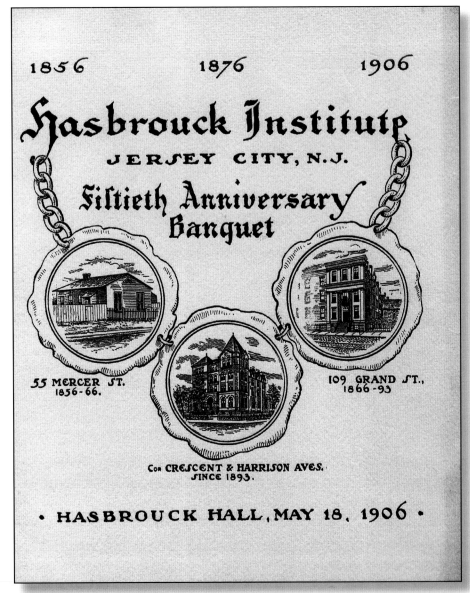

Washington Hasbrouck (c. 1824-1895) founded the Hasbrouck Institute as a preparatory school for young men planning to go to college at 53-55 Mercer Street in 1856. In 1880, a girls' department was added and the curriculum was extended to cover kindergarten through high school. It changed locations as it grew over the years; its final location was a building at Crescent and Harrison avenues from 1893 until its closing in 1912. With the growth of public high school, Jersey City took over the building to create a second high school — Lincoln. The Hasbrouck Institute returned to its separate facilities for boys and girls, housed in private homes. In 1914, the girls' division merged with the Bergen School and a few years later the boys' division closed for good. *Courtesy of the Jersey City Free Public Library.*

There was a time — mid-twentieth century — in Jersey City's history when the Catholic schools educated approximately a quarter of the city's population. Manned primarily by members of religious orders, elementary school classes could be quite large, sometimes numbering upwards of fifty students. This photo shows a group of third graders (c. 1920s) at Saint Anthony's School located downtown. The parish, founded in 1884, was the first in the city devoted to Polish immigrants.

A message from our Blind Girls to you.
St. Joseph's Home Jersey City, N.J.

The Sisters of Saint Joseph of Peace founded the Concordia Learning Center at Saint Joseph's School for the Blind in 1891. It currently serves children who are blind or partially sighted from birth until age 21. In the early years of the school, many charming photos were sent out such as this one showing three little girls and the oldest one reading from a book in Braille.

On August 4, 1882 four young women — Rose Kunz, Margaret Dolan, Mary Storzinger, and Mary Johnson — entered the chapel of Saint Dominic's Academy in bridal dress attended by bridesmaids. The Bishop of Newark, the Right Reverend Winand Michael Wigger (1841-1901), symbolically cut locks of each woman's hair and presented her with the white veil of a novice — the first step in entering a religious order as shown in this August 19, 1882 image from *Frank Leslie's Illustrated Newspaper*.

Saint Dominic Academy was founded in 1878 and has been located at the corner of the Boulevard and Duncan Avenue since 1942. A century later, it still has women dedicated to a life of service. They are members of the Order of Dominican Nuns, founded in Rome in 1218 by Saint Dominic. Nuns from the order also taught at Saint John's Grammar School in the Heights. Shown here on the steps of Saint John's Convent are, left to right, Sister Elizabeth Francis, Sister Grace Margaret, Sister Betty Anne Schultz, Sister Danielle McCarthy (Principal of Saint John's School), Sister Mary Faith, Sister Margaret Thomas (Major Superior of the order) and Sister Adrienne Fallon (Superior at Saint John's).
Courtesy of Saint Dominic Academy.

NEW JERSEY.—RENOUNCING THE WORLD—CANDIDATES FOR ADMISSION TO THE ORDER OF SISTERS OF ST. DOMINIC TAKING THE VAIL AT THE DOMINICAN CONVENT IN JERSEY CITY, AUGUST 4TH.—SEE PAGE 406.

Saint Dominic Academy has been providing a high school education for girls for over a century. In recent years, the Saint Dominic Academy Glee Club has won trophies at national competitions. This view from the rotunda of City Hall shows the students giving a Christmas concert led by Mr. Joseph Natoli.
Photo by Alton O'Neill.

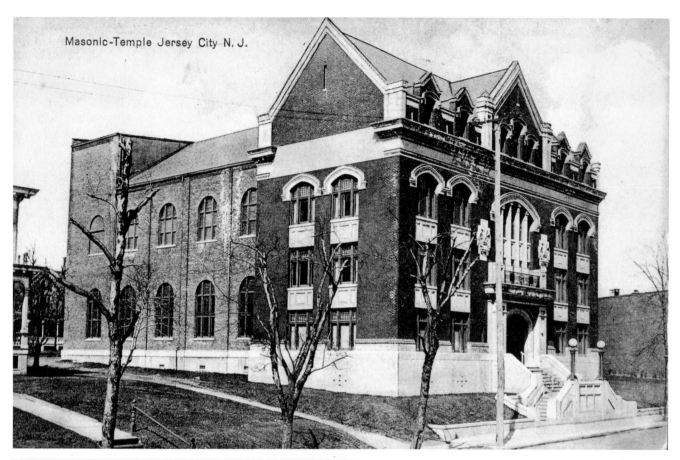

Masonic-Temple Jersey City N. J.

Among the host of organizations and clubs that existed at the beginning of the twentieth century, there were a number of Masonic groups. Freemasonry's Scottish Rite Temple, shown in a c. 1910 postcard, was designed by John T. Rowland, Jr. and opened May 28, 1907. It was given a new lease on life when it was converted into an elementary school for Muslim children. *J. H. Grinnalds, publisher.*

Al Ghazaly Elementary School was established in 1984 and is housed in the former Scottish Rite Temple. As with the religious-based schools previously set up in the city, it seeks to preserve their cultural identity, instill religious teachings, and develop a sense of morality. Al Ghazaly Elementary School provides an Islamic environment that merges New Jersey's Core Curriculum Standards with Qur'an, Islamic Studies, and the Arabic language. Here Mayor Glenn Cunningham speaks to students on the school's campus. *Photo by Alton O'Neill.*

Vocational Schools and Higher Education

Trade schools began to appear, sometimes as an alternative to high school, but increasingly as additional preparation for a career. There was Drake Business School as well as Spencer's. The Medical Center, and Christ and Saint Francis Hospitals, offered schools of nursing.

Jesuit priests established the first college, Saint Peter's, in 1872. The forerunner of New Jersey City University was the school established by the Board of Education shortly before 1870, which provided training for new teachers. It gradually expanded over time from a six-month course to two years and finally, the state chartered it as the New Jersey State Normal School at Jersey City in 1927. In 1929, the school became the first in the country to offer a three-year program, which became four years in 1935. There was a short-lived Jersey City Junior College that offered classes in the evenings at Lincoln High School. Hudson County Community College at Journal Square was founded in 1974.

St. Peter's College, Jersey City, N.J.

Saint Peter's College was chartered by an Act of the Legislature of New Jersey on April 3, 1872. There were three departments established for young men: the college, a high school preparatory school, and a grammar school. The doors opened September 2, 1878 with Father George B. Kenny S. J. (1840-1912) as the first President. The first degrees were awarded June 25, 1889. By 1900, sixty-three Bachelor degrees and twenty-six Masters had been conferred. Eventually each school became a separate entity. Shown in this 1911 Valentine & Sons postcard is the first building erected on Grand Street downtown.

In 1933, the Young property, situated on two and a half acres stretching along Glenwood Avenue and Hudson Boulevard to Montgomery Street, proved to be just what the Jesuits needed to begin building a college campus. E. F. C. Young (1835-1909) and his son Edward L. Young (1861-1940) had elegant and large homes on the property. The father was a powerhouse in Jersey City in the nineteenth century, holding the presidency of many companies including the First National Bank, Dixon Crucible Company, and the New Coaldale Coal Company.

Florence Pond Graham reminisced about the ladies who visited her mother: "I remember my sister and I standing at a window upstairs waiting for Mrs. E. F. C. Young to arrive…it was a never-to-be-forgotten sight to see the footman jump from the box, swing wide the door and assist Mrs. Young up the front stairs."

This picture shows one of the Young family homes on the estate.

Courtesy of Saint Peter's College Archives, Photographic Collection, Jersey City, NJ.

With much of the student body as well as the staff taking up arms during World War I, Saint Peter's College closed. The Preparatory School became the sole occupant of the building since the grammar school had separated and moved to 269 Summit Avenue in 1905. By 1930 it was decided to re-open the college. A new and separate location was needed. The fourth floor of the Chamber of Commerce Building located at 1 Newark Avenue provided an excellent temporary home until an appropriate location for a campus could be acquired. This is a view of the Chamber's building, designed by William Neumann Jr. (1902-1971), while under construction in 1925. *Courtesy of the Jersey City Free Public Library.*

Saint Peter's College Gymnasium, the first building to be constructed, was named for Father Patrick Marley Collins, S. J. (1864-1934) who had died that March 5 after many years of service to the school. At the ground breaking for Collins' gym on September 28, 1934, the young men wearing the beanies are freshmen since the first sophomore class of the newly reopened college determined in 1931 that the first year students should wear blue and white beanies as well as follow the "Freshman Rules," which required submission to the mighty sophomores. Pictured at the groundbreaking are, from left to right, the architect, William Neumann, Jr., Senior Class member, James E. McCormack 1935 (1911-1981), 1915 Alumnus Father Joseph T. Malone (1891-1956), President of the college, Father Joseph S. Dinneen S. J. (1899-1977) holding the spade, the college Dean, Father Robert I. Gannon, S. J. (1893-1978), and Robert Burke who represented the Censullo Burke Construction Company.
Courtesy of Saint Peter's College Archives, Photographic Collection, Jersey City, NJ.

Under Father Victor Yanitelli S. J. (1914-1993), the longest serving President of the college, many strides were made: one of the most notable was the admission of women to the Day Session in 1966, making Saint Peter's College fully coeducational. To this day, improvements continue to be made. For the first century of its existence, it was considered a commuter college. Now there are dormitories and students are recruited from across the country. The recently completed bridge shown here connects the two parts of the campus that are separated by the Boulevard making movement about the university safer.

Christ Hospital was established in 1872 by Rev. Richard M. Abercrombie (1822-1884) of Saint Matthew's Episcopal Church. Over one hundred years ago the hospital established a School of Nursing, which is still in operation today. This photo is of the Class of 1911. Among the graduates was Georgetta Foster Simmons (1887-1981) who, at the time of her death at age 93, was the oldest living graduate of the nursing school.
Courtesy of the Jersey City Free Public Library.

<
Over the years additional buildings have been added to the campus. This sixth major building, Saint Peter's Hall, was constructed as a residence for the Jesuits who had been living in scattered houses around the college. This cornerstone laying ceremony took place May 31, 1959. Then-President of the College, Father James Shanahan (1907-1996) is seen kissing the ring of Archbishop of Newark, the Most Reverend Thomas Boland (1896-1974). Visible is the space within the cornerstone where memorabilia would be sealed away.
Courtesy of Saint Peter's College Archives, Photographic Collection, Jersey City, NJ.

The Jersey City Medical Center and Saint Francis Hospital also offered nursing schools, both of which are no longer in existence. The forerunner of the Medical Center, the Jersey City Hospital established a School of Nursing in 1907. When a broken leg and appendicitis landed Art Wilson in the Jersey City Hospital in 1921, the nurses were kept busy. His whole baseball team visited the ward at once, creating bedlam when one of the players caught his head between the bed's bars. The duty nurse wiped his face with a cold cloth while an orderly applied Vaseline to the panicked boy's head. When he was finally liberated, the nurse bought him a plate of ice cream, stating, "We reserve this for tonsillectomy cases, but you've earned it." When Mayor Hague's Medical Center complex was built, a nurses' residence was included. This is a photo of the graduating class of 1955.
Dan McNulty Collection. Courtesy of the Jersey City Free Public Library.

Social Institutions

Many organizations strive to provide wholesome environments and activities for the people, especially the young, of Jersey City. Religious organizations of various denominations established orphanages in Jersey City and attempted to instill moral character traits through religious classes in Sunday Schools and church-sponsored youth groups. They also tried to insure that marriage was considered a sacred and holy bond to be celebrated. Society, in its largest sense, has, the world over, observed and commemorated marriage. Those customs continue to thrive in Jersey City.

While most of Jersey City's public places and organizations were integrated during the early twentieth century, there were some areas in which there was a distinct separation. One of those areas was the YMCA and YWCA, the Young Men's (and Women's) Christian Association. The YMCA had a large facility on Bergen Avenue and the YWCA on Fairmount Avenue. However, the colored members of both organizations were relegated to storefront branches. The YWCA's House of Friendliness Colored Branch was located at 43 Belmont Avenue while the YMCA's branch was a storefront in the Jackson Avenue vicinity as seen in this c. 1930s photograph. In 1950, the Board of Directors of the YMCA voted for an "open door" policy, ending the separate facility policy that had been in effect since 1919.
Courtesy of the Afro-American Historical Society Museum.

Today young people of every group are welcome at all of the various organizations. One of the most dominant currently is the Boys and Girls Club of Hudson County. It has operated in Jersey City since 1893 and is now located at 1 Canal Street in the downtown section. Its aim is to help "enhance the quality of life for young people and help them recognize and achieve their potential by attaining the skills necessary for living in a complex urban environment." As with all organizations, the Boys and Girls Club has evolved and now houses in part of its facility one of Jersey City's alternative schools, the Learning Community Charter School. This recent rooftop view shows the students of the school assembled to form the initials of the school name.

HOME OF THE HOMELESS, JERSEY CITY.

The Home of the Homeless was located at 366 Grove Street, the former Neilson Homestead. This was one of many orphanages and shelters that existed in Jersey City in the late nineteenth and early twentieth centuries. Established in 1883 as a refuge for destitute women and their children, it remained at this location until 1916 when it moved to a spacious new home at 78 Summit Avenue designed by John T. Rowland, Jr. Another orphanage was Kinderfreund. Jean Becker, whose mother had died leaving an infant son and four little daughters under ten to a husband unable to care for them, wrote a memoir, *An Orphan's Song,* of her years in Kinderfreund, the Lutheran Orphanage at 93 Nelson Avenue in the Heights. A far cry from Oliver Twist, her memories are of kindness exhibited by Father and Mother Sievert, the Protestant minister and his wife who ran the home. At the end of World War II, the orphanage closed; Jean and her siblings found happy homes with their mother's sisters.
Courtesy of the Jersey City Free Public Library.

The Sisters of Saint Joseph of Peace founded an orphanage in Jersey City for Catholic children who were neglected, destitute, abused, or orphaned. When Bishop W. M. Wigger blessed the new orphanage on June 26, 1892, it began with a parade of societies and a drum corps. Located on Grand Street, the five-story building had a playground on the roof; 180 boys and girls settled in upon its opening. These two pictures show some of the little girls and boys who lived there in 1908.
Courtesy of Seton Hall University Archives & Special Collections Center.

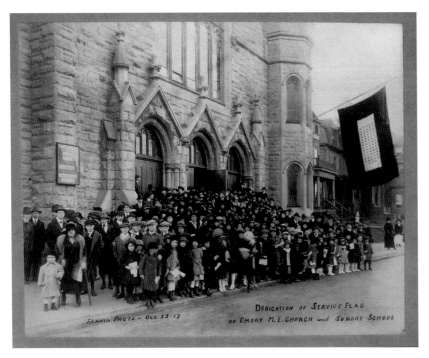

Dedication of Service Flag of Emory M.E. Church and Sunday School
F. Lawin Photo - Oct. 28-17

Once churches were built, the next step taken by Jersey City's clergy was the education of the children. They felt an obligation to help the children, primarily of the poor who were allowed to run undisciplined through the streets. The Protestant leaders worked in a nondenominational effort to establish Sunday Schools. They hosted various excursions, picnics, and parades. It gained such momentum that by the mid-nineteenth century the 1851 Sunday School Parade boasted 1,200 children and three hundred adults marching. Still very strong in the early twentieth century, this photo shows a service flag being presented at Emory Methodist Episcopal Church at Bergen and Belmont avenues. It was customary during World War I for churches to dedicate flags with stars for every church member in the service. *Courtesy of the Jersey City Free Public Library.*

CHAMPIONS Checker Tournament H.C.S.S.A.L. 1914-15

The Hudson County Sunday School Athletic League strove to build character in men and boys through competitive games and meets while maintaining a high standard of honesty and courtesy. Emory ME Church (now Metropolitan AME Church) sponsored this team, which won the checkers championship in the 1914-1915 school year. *Courtesy of the Jersey City Free Public Library.*

Weddings are one of the most joyous of family occasions. From the earliest days, they have been celebrated. Alma Romagnoli (1913-1997), Dickinson High School Class of 1932, married her childhood sweetheart Philip Tosatto (1916-1993), of New York City, October 18, 1936. Alma lived in North Bergen, but North Bergen did not have a high school. Determined to get her education, she often walked from her 8th Street home in North Bergen to Dickinson since she did not have the nickel for the trolley. After the wedding, the newlyweds lived in the Heights. Olga Christiansen (1914-1995) of Ridgefield was Maid of Honor and Edward Wargo, Sr. (1912-1997) of Jersey City was Best Man.

Family and friends of Ignacy (1875-1954) and Malgorzata (1877-1957, nee: Brudnicka) Sławinski came together to mark their 50th Wedding Anniversary exactly fifty years later to the day. Polish immigrants, they were married October 27, 1895 at Saint Anthony of Padua Church in Jersey City. It is the oldest Polish parish in the state of New Jersey. The grand party, complete with a band, was held at White Eagle Hall on Newark Avenue.
Courtesy of Jacqueline Wisner, M.D.

Through the centuries and across cultures, marriage has been and continues to be marked with ceremony and reverence. Here a twenty-first century couple marries in Jersey City in a traditional Asian Indian ceremony.
Photo by Alton O'Neill.

Jersey City's Power Players

Politics is the term for the profession of governing a geographical unit. It is the social mechanism by which people obtain power and authority over others. Our political realm is a democracy in which candidates attempt to convince the populace that they are best suited to administer government. Jersey City and Hudson County have the dubious honor of being known historically as a hotbed of political corruption. Consequently, the area has long been the brunt of humor, often from outside the County. Several elected officials, including three Jersey City mayors and the Hudson County executive, have been convicted and received prison sentences during the twentieth century for their corrupt shenanigans. The predecessor of the telephone book was the city directory—first issued in Jersey City in 1849—that listed every head of household along with their address and occupation. Jersey City folklore says that Frank Hague put an end to the directories after the 1925 edition. It would not bode well for the Political Machine if the opposition had an accurate listing of the residents. Ballot stuffing and "vote early, vote often, dead or alive" could not so easily thrive. But Jersey City has survived—and thrived—both in spite of and thanks to those who have been elected to lead us.

Dudley Sanford Gregory (1800-1874) had the honor of being the first Mayor of Jersey City. After spending his young adulthood in New York, he moved to Jersey City in 1834. Gregory held the mayoral office for three non-consecutive terms starting in 1838. He did much to transform Jersey City into a major industrial center with influence in economic, social, and political spheres. As the first mayor, he had to deal with many challenges, from filling in marshes to guiding various municipal agencies in their infancy. Among his accomplishments, Gregory was director of sixteen railroads, championed public education, and was both a Chosen Freeholder and a United States Representative in Congress. Gregory had many interests and was heavily invested in various enterprises, which made it possible for him to loan his friend Horace Greeley (1811-1872) $1,000. With this financing, Greeley was able to start his newspaper *The Herald Tribune*. Far less well-known about Dudley Gregory is the fact that he attempted to alleviate the worm and insect problem that was plaguing Jersey City. His solution was to bring from England the predator of the worm, that little brown bird we know as the sparrow. *Courtesy of Jersey City Free Public Library.*

For Mayor.
Mark M Fagan.

Third term 1905

For Mayor.
Archibald M Henry
Make Jersey City Prosper
With a Business Administration

Without radio, television, or the Internet, politicians had only personal appearances, newspapers, and the mail to get their names and faces familiar to the electorate. Mailings of political postcards touting a candidate — like these two Real Photo Postcards — were common in 1905 when the bespectacled undertaker, Mark Fagan (1869-1955), a Republican, successfully ran for his third term as Jersey City's Mayor in 1905 against Democratic businessman Archibald Henry (1863-1933).

Exactly one hundred years later in 2005, the two candidates, Judge Jerramiah Healy and former City Council woman Melissa Holloway (1961-2008) — both Democrats — produced postcard-like handouts to promote their candidacies. While having a greater array of public relation tools at their disposal, the simple picture and message is still a powerful tool, to which Mayor Healy, the winner in the election, can attest.

<
At this April 21, 1945 dinner honoring Mary Norton (1875-1959), Frank Hague proclaimed, "She is a great legislator, a great leader and has reflected great credit on the Democratic Party in Hudson County, the State of New Jersey, and the United States."
When women's suffrage was achieved, Hague had tapped Mary to organize the women of Hudson County politically. She went on to many firsts: first Democratic woman to be elected to the Hudson County Board of Freeholders, first Democratic woman elected to Congress without first being preceded by a husband, and first woman elected from an eastern state.
Courtesy of the Jersey City Free Public Library.

>
In 1940, the Republican Party supported Wendell Willkie (1892-1944) as their candidate for President against Franklin D. Roosevelt. He is shown at an October 7 appearance at Journal Square where a crowd of thousands had gathered. He lambasted Frank Hague as a dictator. In a speech made earlier that day in Newark, he spoke almost exclusively of Mayor Hague and the issue of bossism. One of the points that brought cheers for him — and boos for Hague — was the relating of an incident in which the New Jersey Legislature requested the poll books from Hudson County for a review of questionable voting practices and it was informed that they had been burned.
Courtesy of the Jersey City Free Public Library.

The later years of the twentieth century have seen the arrival in large numbers of various Asian and Arab groups. In addition to proclamations, Jersey City also has a ceremony for each individual ethnic group in which the flag of the group's home country is flown over City Hall for a week. After the outdoor ceremony, a celebration is held inside City Hall. Shown are some very exuberant representatives of the Philippino community as they celebrate their homeland.
Photo by Alton O'Neill.

Jersey City has been home to many waves of immigration beginning with the Dutch and English in the 1600s. By the end of the nineteenth century, Germans, Irish, Italian, Polish, and Jewish groups from various eastern European countries immigrated in vast numbers. Mid-twentieth century saw an influx of Puerto Ricans followed by Cubans when Castro took control of their country. Since then Hispanic immigrants from just about every Latino country have added to the cultural blend that is Jersey City. The City tries to recognize the different groups with proclamations and citations such as this one at City Hall showing Mayor Glenn Cunningham flanked by leaders of the Hispanic community. Shown here are Sonia Araujo, Eliau Rivera, Adin Figueroa, Sandra Bolden Cunningham, and Anthony Cruz.
Photo by Alton O'Neill.

Tragedy, fire, and accidents — such events bring out crowds. The Jersey City Fire Department was not established as a for-pay municipal service until June 1871. Prior to that, volunteers performed the job. This etching is of the burning of Prospect Hall at the intersection of Washington, Hudson, and Palisade avenues, which have been changed to Storms, Jewett, and Summit avenues respectively. The quarters on the second floor had been serving as the City Hall for the Town of Bergen when the fire occurred in 1867. It temporarily relocated to Belmont Hall at Monticello Avenue, then to the newly constructed Library Hall. In the pre-dawn hours of June 12, the fire began leaving the building in ashes by 7 a.m. The firemen employed an assembly line-like procedure as a crowd of onlookers gathered.
Courtesy of the Jersey City Free Public Library.

The police, like the firemen, must act quickly and take command of any situation in which life or property is endangered. This c. 1940s accident on then-Hudson Boulevard was photographed from the porch of 3709. Crowds line the street on both sides to view the wrecked truck and its removal. At that time, the Boulevard, which was constructed in 1894, requiring the removal or demolition of many homes, had its own police force. In 1966, the Kennedy Boulevard and the Hudson County police departments were consolidated to decrease county costs, but then phased out entirely in 1996. Today the Jersey City Police Department handles accidents like this one. *Photo by Alma Tosatto.*

This c. 1938 cartoon citing eight different scenarios for voting fraud — from babies to corpses voting, from ballot stuffing to using fifty different names — appeared in *The New York Post*. The local papers in Hudson County were heavily discouraged from opposing the Political Machine. When *The Jersey Journal* began to challenge his tactics, even referring to his followers as "Hague's Hoodlums," the Mayor almost destroyed the paper. Among his strategies were discouraging advertisers, leaning on shopkeepers who sold the paper, and even officially having the name of Journal Square changed to Veterans' Square by ordinance in 1928. The people, however, had different ideas and, to this day, refer to it as Journal Square. *Courtesy of the Jersey City Free Public Library.*

This 2004 political cartoon by Jimmy Margulies, whose work appears in major publications across the country, including the *Washington Post* and the *New York* and *Los Angeles Times,* alludes to one of the reasons why Hudson County has had such a reputation for corruption; it gives testimony to a notoriety that goes beyond local borders. *Courtesy of Jimmy Margulies.*

Yours very truly
Benjamin C Taylor

One of the earliest published books about Jersey City's history is *The Annals of the Classis of Bergen of the Reformed Dutch Church...including the Civil History of the Ancient Township of Bergen.* The third edition was published in 1857. It was written by the pastor of the church, Benjamin C. Taylor, DD (1801-1881). *Winfield, 1874.*

Charles Hardenburg Winfield (1829-1898) wrote *History of Land Titles in Hudson County, NJ 1609-1871* in 1872 and *History of the County of Hudson, New Jersey: From its Earliest Settlement to the Present Time* in 1874. *Courtesy of the Jersey City Free Public Library.*

Chapter Six:

The Keepers of History

Were it not for the foresight of those who came before us, we would not have the windows to the past that we have today. Among the most prominent of those keepers of history are Benjamin C. Taylor (1801-1881), Charles Winfield (1829-1898), Alexander McLean (c. 1846-1916), and Daniel Van Winkle (1839-1935) who wrote large volumes of the history about the city and Hudson County. William Richardson (1864-1937), J. Owen Grundy (1911-1985), Theodore Conrad (1910-1994), and Glenn Cunningham (1943-2004) regularly wrote articles for the local papers.

Recent works by Joan Doughty Lovero, Barbara Petrick, Robert Leach, Patrick Shahloub, Carmela Karnoutsos, Kenneth French, Randall Gabrielan, Charles Caldes, and Teddy Goral continue to fascinate the countless number of folks with ties to the City. There are many more writers of various aspects of life in Jersey City — some who have produced books, magazine or newspaper articles, documentaries, and so much more. A bibliography of such items could produce a small tome in itself.

Organizations have also been vital in the preservation process. Shortly after Abraham Lincoln's assassination in 1865, the Lincoln Association was formed. The Jersey City Free Public Library, established in 1889, plays a large and invaluable role in the preservation of Jersey City's history. In 1908, the Library established the Hudson County Historical Society, which collected many wonderful documents, books, photos, maps, and other artifacts. They are housed in the New Jersey Room in the Main Library. The Library also houses the Afro-American Historical Society Museum in its Greenville Branch and was the creator of the now autonomous Jersey City Museum.

Even now, in the twenty-first century, maybe even more than in the past, the citizenry is acutely aware of the need to research and preserve history. The birth of the new Millennium has seen several new history-oriented organizations blossom. In 1999, John Gomez founded the Jersey City Landmarks Conservancy. With him at the helm, it established its goal "to preserve, protect, and promote Jersey City's irreplaceable historic resources." It sponsors Preservation Month every May, hosting tours, clean-ups, panel discussions, and workshops.

An offshoot of the Landmarks Conservancy is S.A.V.E. — Sustaining Architectural Vitality in the Environment — a youth advocacy group operating under the auspices of the Conservancy. Finally, the Hudson County Genealogical Society was formed in 2007. It plans meetings at historic sites such as the Beacon (the former Medical Center) and the Brennan Court House. Already its membership has grown to well over one hundred with members from coast to coast representing twenty states.

Finally, let us not forget the legion of reporters who wrote for *The Evening Journal* (now *The Jersey Journal)*, the *Jersey City News*, the *Argus*, the *Observer*, the *Hudson Dispatch*, and the many other newspapers and periodicals that existed during the last two centuries. What they wrote on a daily basis as news has been a written history for us. Among those who currently seek out historic topics upon which to write are John Gomez of *The Jersey Journal* and Ricardo Kaulessar of the weekly *Jersey City Reporter*.

This C. T. Harris photo of 46 Bentley Avenue was Florence Pond Graham's childhood home. She describes much of life throughout her childhood and teenage years in her book *Jersey City As I Remember It*. Her first memory was of walking over a plank in what was to be the dining room in their new home on Bentley Avenue while it was being constructed. The house, built c. 1898, is still lovely today.

This C. T. Harris photo of 2 Wegman Court is the first home that Art Wilson's parents owned. The Wilson family purchased its first car, a used Buick, after World War I, and Art's father Sam single-handedly excavated the cellar, which was two-thirds underground, made a concrete driveway, and thus built a garage for their Buick. The Wilsons moved there from 231 Bidwell Avenue when Art was five years old. After Art's freshman year at Lincoln High School, the family moved to East Orange. In 2005, the home was transferred from the Hudson County Sheriff to HUD. There have been two subsequent owners, but it now stands forlorn and boarded up.

In 1908, the Jersey City Free Public Library selected a committee to organize a historical society; thus, the Hudson County Historical Society was born. An active group for almost fifty years, it celebrated grandly at this magnificent dinner held at the Scottish Rite Temple on Park Street October 20, 1910. It was the culminating activity in the citywide celebration commemorating the 250th Anniversary of the establishment of Bergen, the original name of what is now Jersey City.
Courtesy of the Jersey City Free Public Library.

Every year since its inception, the Lincoln Association has honored our fallen President on the anniversary of his birth, February 12, with a dinner, no matter the weather. This dinner, on February 12, 1952, was at the Hotel Plaza in Journal Square.
Dan McNulty Collection. Courtesy of the Jersey City Free Public Library.

One hundred years later, the Jersey City Landmarks Conservancy celebrates the successes of those who value the history and preservation of Jersey City. Each year the organization recognizes the achievements of those who work to preserve history whether in the architectural or cultural form. The JCLC holds an annual awards ceremony at the historic Loew's Theatre at Journal Square every May. This picture is taken from the balcony during a recent ceremony.
Courtesy of Ken Clare, 2006.

In 1964, the Jersey City Free Public Library established a separate department — the New Jersey Room — for the purpose of organizing, preserving, and making accessible the wide array of materials related to local history. The managers of the department since the 1970s are assembled, in order of their tenure, in front of glass-door bookcases installed in 1900. Pictured June 12, 2001 at the reopening of the department after renovations are from right to left: Joan Doherty Lovero, Patrick Shalhoub, Kenneth French, and this book's author, Cynthia Harris.
Courtesy of Bernard Harris.

In 1977, the Afro-American Historical and Cultural Society Museum was organized by Captain Thomas Taylor (1926-2009), President of the local chapter of the NAACP, Theodore Brunson, Nora Fant (1903-1987), and Virginia Dunnaway (1925-2007). It has worked hard to discover and highlight what historian Glenn Cunningham termed the "hidden footprints" of Jersey City — the African American presence here since early times. The Society's scope goes beyond the city's borders. Housed on the second floor of the Greenville Branch of the Jersey City Free Public Library and currently directed by Ted's son Neal Brunson, this picture shows a doll exhibit above which is a genealogical chart of one of Jersey City's early prominent black families, the Jacksons. They owned extensive property prior to the Civil War.
Photo by Alton O'Neill.

Robert Leach of the Historical Project is a raconteur, enchanting audiences with his wealth of anecdotes about Jersey City's most famous mayor, Frank "I am the Law" Hague. He has produced several books, CDs, and DVDs of captivating tales of Jersey City such as *The Eyes of Saint Joseph*. He is seated besides retired attorney Richard Vaughn, who is holding a small portion of Richard's collection of political posters, buttons, and portraits of local dignitaries that were donated to the New Jersey Room of the Jersey City Free Public Library.
Photo by Alton O'Neill.

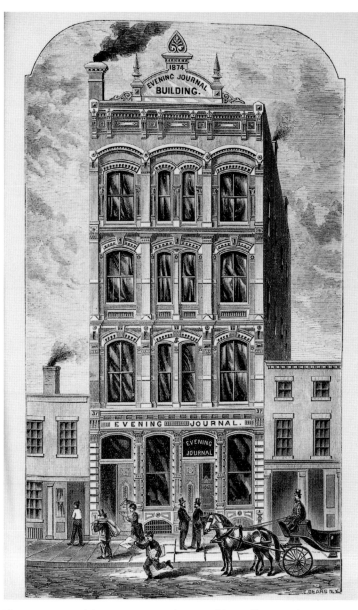

There were several dozen newspapers that served Jersey City over the years, some weekly or twice a week and some daily but short lived. The three most enduring were dailies. The *Jersey (or Hudson) Observer* ran from 1904-1951, the *Hudson Dispatch* (a weekly in the nineteenth century) ran from 1900-1991, and *The Jersey Journal* (originally *The Evening Journal*) was begun in 1867. This was *The Jersey Journal's* third home constructed in the mid-1870s. Like the first two locations, it was also located downtown at 37 Montgomery Street. *Farrier, 1879.*

Initially published in the evening and named *The Evening Journal* in 1867, Jersey City's longest running daily newspaper changed its name to *The Jersey Journal* in 1909. After occupying several downtown locations from 1867 to 1911 and then moving uptown to Bergen and Sip Avenues, *The Jersey Journal* moved to its present location, a building designed by prolific architect John T. Rowland, Jr., at 30 Journal Square in 1925.

William H. Richardson (1864-1937) wrote extensively during the first three decades of the twentieth century during which he was Jersey City's historian. "The Richardson Papers," which include his correspondence, historical commemoration plans, and writings, are housed in the New Jersey Room of the Main Library. He often disputed the facts as presented in written articles by such publications as National Geographic with lively exchanges of correspondence. *Courtesy of the Jersey City Free Public Library.*

John Gomez, shown in this C. T. Harris photo, has continued the tradition of keeping Jersey City history alive with exciting stories of the often little-known backgrounds of people and places integral to Jersey City history. His column "Legends and Landmarks" appears in *The Jersey Journal*. A middle school teacher in Jersey City with a Master of Science in Historic Preservation from Columbia University, John is uniquely qualified to guide fellow preservationists in what needs to be done in Jersey City.

J. Owen Grundy (1911-1985) was a prolific writer for a large part of the century until his 1985 death. He wrote a column for *The Jersey Journal*. Owen kept meticulous and copious notes on a wide range of subjects significant to Jersey City. A pier on the waterfront and an impressive boardroom in the Main Library are named in his honor.
Courtesy of the Jersey City Free Public Library.

Over the course of Jersey City's life there have been over forty daily or weekly newspapers with countless reporters, much of whose words are still available to us today via the microfilmed papers. Reporters have always been driven to "get the scoop." Here reporters from the three dailies — *The Jersey Journal*, the *Hudson Observer*, and the *Hudson Dispatch* — as well as a New York City reporter, eagerly scribble down the words of Frank Hague, Jersey City's Mayor for an unprecedented thirty years from 1917 to 1947.
Courtesy of the Jersey City Free Public Library.

Sixty years later, still with pad in hand, *The Jersey Journal*'s veteran reporter Earl Morgan takes notes as he speaks with Mayor Glenn Cunningham at the groundbreaking ceremonies for a new regional library branch in 2003. The Mayor's Director of Communications, Stan Eason, listens.
Photo by Alton O'Neill.

Not all the recording of history was with words. August Will (1834-1910) was a talented artist who sketched and painted Jersey City as it appeared in the latter half of the nineteenth century. The Jersey City Free Public Library purchased 127 of his views, which are now part of the Jersey City Museum's collection. Thus, his wish that his "most treasured possession," the documentation of the city's growth, be available for the public's edification and education was realized. The scenes were bucolic with lush vegetation and wide, open spaces. They are visual images of a time long past.
Courtesy of the Jersey City Free Public Library.

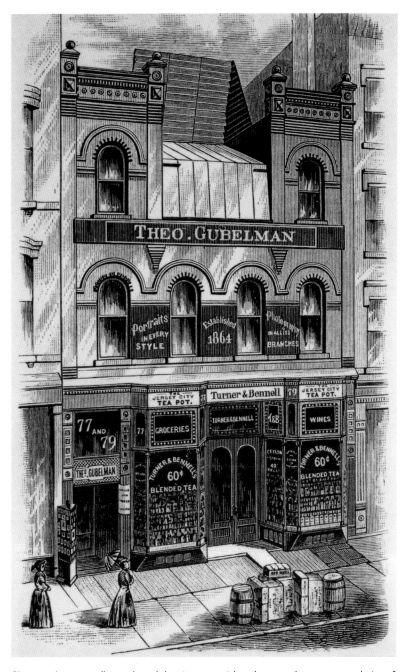

Photography eventually supplanted drawing as a quick and extremely accurate rendering of people and places. Jersey City had, in the nineteenth century, dozens of photographers listed in the city directories. Theodore Gubelman established his business in early 1864 and was one of the most productive and creative, equally at home with both portraiture and landscape photography. Shown is his studio at 77-79 Montgomery Street. *McLean, 1895.*

JERSEY CITY
LANDMARKS
CONSERVANCY

S.A.V.E. was founded by high school students who emulate the work of the Conservancy and strive to raise awareness, participate in preservation initiatives, and inspire other young people to embrace the cause. On June 13, 2007, the Jersey City Municipal Council passed a resolution recognizing S.A.V.E. as an official youth advocacy organization. Front row, on bench seat, are Janita Sawh, Stephanie Castano, and Eunice Martins; Second row, on bench back, are Aaron Haier, Janika Berridge, and Helene Chen; not pictured are Ruby Hankey and Violet Malolepsza.
Photo by C. T. Harris.

A grassroots campaign succeeded in saving the Hudson and Manhattan Powerhouse from the wrecking ball. The imminent destruction of this magnificent structure, built in 1908, was the catalyst that led to the creation of the Jersey City Landmarks Conservancy in 1999. Through its efforts the Powerhouse is now on the National Register of Historic Places and the Conservancy will continue to monitor its eventual redevelopment. The Powerhouse has become the symbol of the JCLC and has been incorporated into its logo as seen here.
Courtesy of the Jersey City Landmarks Conservancy.

It is to these young people and all the subsequent generations who will call Jersey City home that we entrust the safekeeping of our history. Hold on to it fast with all your hearts.

Bibliography

A & P History, http://www.aptea.com/history.asp

Abbott, Lynn and Doug Seroff. *Black Traveling Shows, Coon Songs and the Dark Pathway to Blues and Jazz*. Jackson, Mississippi: University Press of Mississippi, 2007.

Ballou's Pictorial. Boston, Massachusetts: May 23, 1857.

City Directories for Jersey City.

Dear, Joseph A., ed. 1929. *The Book of New Jersey*. Jersey City, New Jersey: Jersey City Printing Company.

Dickenson, Richard. "A Blackwood Look at Jackson Lane, A Greenville, Jersey City Street," 1975.

Eaton, Harriet Phillips. *Jersey City and Its Historic Sites*. Jersey City, New Jersey: Jersey City Woman's Club, 1899

Farrier, George H., Ed. *Memorial of the Centennial Celebration of the Battle of Paulus Hook, August 19th, 1879 With a History of the Early Settlement and Present Condition of Jersey City, NJ*. Jersey City, New Jersey: M. Mullone Printer, 1879.

Forepaugh's Circus (http://en.wikipedia.org/wiki/Adam_Forepaugh)

Francisco, Charles. *The Radio City Music Hall: An Affectionate History of the World's Greatest Theater*. New York, New York: E. P. Dutton, 1979.

Gabrielan, Randall. *Jersey City, A Monumental History*. Atglen, Pennsylvania: Schiffer Publishing, Ltd., 2007.

Gomez, John. "Legends and Landmarks." *The Jersey Journal*. Jersey City, New Jersey: various dates.

Graham, Florence Pond. *Jersey City: As I Remember It*. United States of America, 1964.

Hudson County Genealogical Society (http://www.hudsoncountynjgenealogy.org/)

Hudson Dispatch, Union City, New Jersey; multiple dates.

Illustrated Christian Weekly. New York, New York: November 7, 1874

Jersey City. Jersey City, New Jersey: Chamber of Commerce, multiple dates.

Jersey City Division of Planning, unpublished archives.

Jersey City Hospital, School of Nursing, The Golden Years, 1957

Jersey City Landmarks Conservancy (http://www.jclandmarks.org/)

Jersey Journal, The (previously *The Evening Journal*), multiple dates.

Jersey Observer, The (previously *The Hudson Observer*), multiple dates.

Leach, Bob, ed. *Jersey City Landmarks*. Jersey City, New Jersey: City of Jersey City, 2000

Leach, Bob. *The Frank Hague Picture Book*. Jersey City, New Jersey: Jersey City Historical Project, Jersey City Free Public Library, 1998.

Lincoln High School. *The Quill*. Jersey City, New Jersey, June 1950.

Lovero, Joan Doherty. *Hudson County, The Left Bank*. Sun Valley, California: American Historical Press, 1999.

Lurie, Maxine and Marc Mappen, ed. *Encyclopedia of New Jersey*. New Brunswick, New Jersey: Rutgers University Press, 2004.

McLean, Alexander. *History of Jersey City, NJ: A Record of Its Early Settlement and Corporate Progress*. Jersey City, New Jersey: Jersey City Printing Co., 1895.

Mott, Jacolyn A., ed. *Heroes in the Fight for Beauty: The Muralists of the Hudson County Court House*. Jersey City, New Jersey: Jersey City Museum, 1985

New Jersey City University. "Jersey City: Past and Present." (http://www.njcu.edu/programs/jchistory/entries.html)

New York Times. New York, New York: multiple dates

Petrick, Barbara Burns. *Church and School in the Immigrant City: A Social History of Public Education in Jersey City, 1804-1930*. Metuchen, New Jersey: Upland Press, 2000.

Saint Peter's College. *Peacock Pie*. Jersey City, New Jersey: 1972.

Saint Peter's Preparatory School. *Petrean*. Jersey City, New Jersey: 1974.

Scientific American. New York, New York: February 27, 1875 and February 20, 1886

Shriners of North America (http://www.shrinershq.org/Shrine/)

Sustaining Architectural Vitality in the Environment (S.A.V.E.) — http://savearchitecture.org/

Sweetland, David R. *Erie Railroad in Color*. Edison, New Jersey: Morning Sun Books, 1991.

Taylor, Benjamin C. *Annals of the Classis of Bergen of the Reformed Dutch Church and of the Churches Under its Care: Included The Civil History of the Ancient Township of Bergen in New Jersey*. New York, New York: Board of Publications of the Reformed Protestant Dutch Church, 1857.

Vernon, Leonard F. *Images of America: Jersey City Medical Center*. Charleston, South Carolina: Arcadia Publishing, 2004.

Wilson, Art. *No Experience Required: Bumbling through Boyhood*. Cambria, California: Dead Reckoning Press, 1984.

Winfield, Charles H. *History of the County of Hudson, New Jersey*. New York, New York: Kennard & Hay Stationery Manufacturing and Printing Company, 1874.

Index